2-

essential

essential

GUITAR

From Bach to Rock—Everything You Need
to Master Your Favorite Instrument

Jack Wilkins and Peter Rubie

Adams Media Corporation
Avon, Massachusetts

Published by Adams Media, an F+W Publications Company
57 Littlefield Street, Avon, MA 02322 U.S.A.
www.adamsmedia.com

ISBN: 1-59869-136-8

Printed by KHL Printing Co Pte Ltd, in Singapore.

J I H G F E D C B A

This publication is designed to provide accurate and authoritative information with regard to the subject matter covered. It is sold with the understanding that the publisher is not engaged in rendering legal, accounting, or other professional advice. If legal advice or other expert assistance is required, the services of a competent professional person should be sought.
—From a *Declaration of Principles* jointly adopted by a Committee of the American Bar Association and a Committee of Publishers and Associations

Many of the designations used by manufacturers and sellers to distinguish their products are claimed as trademarks. Where those designations appear in this book and Adams Media was aware of a trademark claim, the designations have been printed with initial capital letters.

Illustrations by Barry Littmann.
Photographs courtesy of Peter Abréu.
Music typesetting by Woytek Rynczak of WR Music Service.
Special thanks to Adam Sabalewski for providing a technical review.

Contents

Introduction
Peter Rubie

Though the guitar has been around since the Stone Age, we think of it more as a twentieth-century instrument—from the turn-of-the-century concert hall performances of Segovia, to the rural blues mythology of Robert Johnson (who played so movingly it was said he had sold his soul to the Devil for the gift), to the startling electric jazz guitar of Charlie Christian, and on to the arrival of brilliant and outlandish rock guitarists such as Jimi Hendrix in the 1960s.

The guitar itself is a remarkable instrument. The six strings of the guitar have a musical range of more than three octaves, more than half that achieved by a piano, and the strings can be sounded together, giving the guitar the sense of being a small orchestra. It is more intimate and in some ways more responsive to a player's mood than almost any other instrument, and has both a pure singing soprano as well as a resonant bass—not bad for a musical instrument three feet long and weighing less than most housecats.

FACTS

The guitar has many forebears and cousins—the lute, the Middle Eastern *oud,* the Indian *sitar,* the banjo, the *koto* of Japan, the *bouzouki* of Greece, the *vihuela,* the *yue-chin, chirar, balalaika, rehab, kayakeum, santir, ombi, vambi, nanga, samisen* . . . and on and on.

Guitar players number more self-taught musicians among their ranks than those of almost any other instrument. That's because it is easy to play simply, and very difficult to play well. Unlike other instrumentalists, guitarists are infamous for not being able to read music well. In fact, a joke among musicians goes: How do you get guitar players to stop playing? The answer: Put a sheet of music in front of them and make them read it.

In this book, we will introduce you to an amazing instrument that has more personalities and ways to make music than possibly any other, and give you some ideas and suggestions about that variety. We'll give you ideas on what to practice, how to practice, and which great guitarists you should listen to—and Jack Wilkins, the coauthor of this book, is one of the first and finest.

But most of all, you should practice a little bit every day, even if it's for only ten minutes, and don't worry if it doesn't sound good, or you think it's all wrong. The key is consistency. Despite the sore fingertips, keep at it; it will all come right eventually.

If you can play a musical instrument, the personal rewards are wondrous. If you're lucky, your guitar and your music will take you around the world and into the homes and cafés and hearts of people with whom you may have little else in common except the language of music. And that is truly something worth striving for. I know, because it has guided my life into some of its best and most profound moments. Music has bonded me in the best way to my brother, who owns a jazz club and is himself a wonderful musician in London; it introduced me to three great teachers, the jazz bass player and philosopher Peter Ind, and the jazz saxophone players Warne Marsh and George Coleman; and it has given me friends in many countries, including my best friend, coauthor Jack Wilkins, whose mastery of the guitar is breathtaking. Find his records and CDs, listen to them, and then find the records and CDs of the other players we discuss in this book. Finally, music gave me its greatest gift, my wife, Melody, a gifted musician and teacher in her own right.

I hope that music gives you at least half the gifts and joys it has given me. Despite the frustrations and difficulties, it will be well worth it. Trust me.

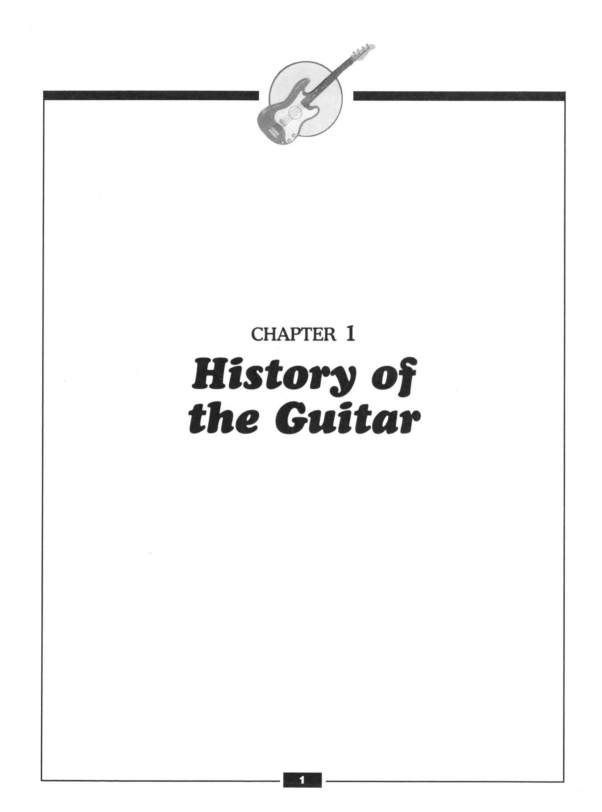

CHAPTER 1

History of the Guitar

In the Beginning . . .

The guitar, or something a lot like it, has been around since the dawn of time. One day, a Stone Age hunter stuck the end of his bow into his mouth and started twanging the bowstring. And so the guitar was born. This is not just a wild guess. The first picture we have of the "guitar" is in Trois Frères, in the south of France. In a Paleolithic cave painting, a figure is seen wearing a mask with a bow fastened to it. He holds the instrument in his left hand and plucks it with his right. A similar instrument, called the *okongo* or *cora,* is still used in parts of Africa to this day.

Early Forms of the Guitar

In the pre-Christian Babylonian, Egyptian, and Hittite cultures of the Middle East, and on through Roman Italy, Greece, and Turkey in the Near East, varying types of stringed instruments developed with certain aspects in common. Each had some sort of sound box, long necks, and chords or strings that were stretched over the sound box and along the neck and fastened at one end. As players used one hand to strum (perhaps with a plectrum of some sort), and the other to stop the strings at various points along the neck, they could sound a wide variety of notes, both singly and together. Around 1400 B.C., for example, there is evidence that the Hittites played a four-stringed guitarlike instrument that had a characteristic figure-eight rounded shape.

FACTS

Apollo, the Greek god of archers, is also, by a strange quirk of fate, the god of music. His lyre was composed of a turtle shell, with strings made of sheep gut or fiber stretched across.

The Evolution of the Modern Guitar
The Four-Course Guitar

The Romans brought their *tanbur* or *cithara* to Spain around A.D. 400. In the eighth century, the conquering Arab Moors introduced the *ud.* By the thirteenth century, there are a number of references and pictures of guitarlike instruments throughout Europe. It is possible that makers of the Roman-style *cithara* and the Arabic *ud* influenced one another, so that by A.D. 1200, the four-string guitar had evolved into two types: the *guitarra morisca* (Moorish guitar), which had a pear-shaped, rounded back, a wide fingerboard, and several sound holes somewhat like a lute; and the *guitarra latina* (Latin guitar), which resembled a small version of the modern guitar, with one sound hole and a narrower neck. This early instrument was a "four-course" guitar, and it is the likely forerunner of the modern ukulele. (Each pair of strings was called a *course*.)

By 1487, Johannes Tinctoris described a Spanish instrument called the *vihuela,* whose sides "curved inward on both sides," and another instrument invented by the people of Catalonia, "which some call the *guiterra* and others the *ghiterne*." He added that because "of the thinness of its sound . . . it was being used much more often by women to accompany love songs, than by men." In Italy, these instruments were known as the *viola da mano* and *chitarra.*

The Six-Course Guitar

While the *guiterra* was small and had four courses, the *chitarra* was larger and had six courses. Both had thongs or chords tied at various places along the neck to make frets or squarelike divisions of the neck. They became the instrument of choice for wandering troubadours or minstrels, who were virtual one-man bands, having to master pipes, whistles, flutes, songs, storytelling, and anything else that would earn them money and keep them from facing the displeasure of aggravated patrons.

FACTS

Minstrels did not use the "guitars" to accompany their stories, but to play small instrumental interludes between verses or tales or to sing folksongs.

Here's how a Swiss poet named Amarcius described a minstrel's performance in the eleventh century: "When the citharist appears, after arranging for his fee, and proceeds to remove his instrument from its cover of oxhide, the people assemble from far and near, fix their eyes upon him and listen with soft murmurs as he strikes the strings with his fingers stretched far apart, strings which he himself has fashioned from sheep gut, and which he plays now tenderly, now with harsh booming sounds."

The Lute

The lute held sway as the major stringed instrument for a long while, but it had a number of drawbacks. First of all, there was no standard lute, so some were large, and some smaller, some had eight strings, others twelve or even more, and they were the absolute devil both to play and to keep in tune.

Soon after the reign of King Henry VIII in England, around 1550, the guitar had begun to become a more popular stringed instrument, but for some time to come, rival camps of lutenists and guitarists would lose no opportunity to badmouth the others' instrument and musicianship. In 1556 in France, for example, it was reported that while the pear-shaped lute had been a popular instrument, people were playing the guitar even more.

FACTS

A keen musician himself (and rumored to be the composer of "Greensleeves"), King Henry had more than twenty guitars among his collection of musical instruments in Hampton Court Palace.

Compositions for the Guitar

The earliest known music for the guitar was written for the *vihuela*. "El Maestro" by Luis Milan, a Spaniard, was published in 1535 for the use and enjoyment of Spanish courtiers and aristocracy. Seven books of music survive, written in tablature. This early form of music is a sort of diagram showing each string of the guitar and indicating where it should be stopped along the neck. Above the diagrams are notes indicating time values, or how long each note should be sounded. The diagrams show pieces of varying degrees of difficulty, including a series of regal dances known as *pavanes*.

Ten years later, Alonso Mudarra published a music book called *Tres Libros de Musica en Cifras para Vihuela.* This book contains several sophisticated, sometimes even dissonant, pieces that include a recurrent bass line which gives the music a syncopated, energetic feel.

By the early seventeenth century, there were a number of books and tutors on playing the guitar, particularly in France, where the instrument had become popular. Adaptations of lute music and arrangements of dances and fantasias encouraged the use of the guitar as a member of an ensemble or as an accompaniment to songs.

FACTS

Early guitars had gut strings in courses or pairs, with a variety of tunings. A four-course guitar had ten frets and was often tuned to either FCEA, GCEA, or CFAD. The top three strings were tuned in unison, while the bass string (either F or G) was tuned in octaves, or eight notes apart.

The music of this period was not played as rigidly structured as classical music is today. There was room for improvisation, particularly when it came to variations of melodic phrasing and ornamentation. Advanced players, as always, could perform florid single-note passages and counterpoint and figured bass runs. Generally, however, the fashion for most players of the guitar at this time was for rather basic playing, mainly strummed chord patterns.

By 1600, the five-course guitar had replaced the earlier four-course and six-course guitars. The tuning also became more standardized, predominantly ADGBE. The Italian guitarist Giovanni Paolo Foscarini wrote some sophisticated new pieces for the instrument in the 1630s, while a fellow countryman, Francesco Corbetta, became one of the foremost virtuosos on the guitar, traveling widely throughout Europe, popularizing the instrument.

Many Musical Modifications

At the end of the Baroque period, two significant changes had occurred. The five courses were replaced by six single strings, and they were tuned in the modern style of EADGBE. Toward the end of the eighteenth century, Federico Moretti wrote the first standardized book on the six-string guitar, *The Principles of Playing the Guitar with Six Strings* (1799).

Many changes were taking place musically by this time. The modern piano first appeared, and as it did, the guitar began to fade from popularity and was considered a more frivolous instrument of seduction and amour. A German diarist wrote, "The flat guitar with its strum we shall happily leave to the garlic-eating Spaniards."

Romance, lasciviousness, and the guitar have been fairly consistent partners for a while, not just in the modern age of heavy-metal rockers. For example, Ronsard, a famous French poet of the fifteenth century wrote:

> *It is the ideal instrument*
> *For ladies of great learning,*
> *Lascivious ladies also play*
> *To advertise their yearning.*

Gaspar Sanz, guitarist to the viceroy of Aragon, Spain, was as much a philosopher as a musician. His comments about the instrument and its players stands as well today as it did when he wrote the introduction to his method book on the guitar in the late seventeenth century: "[The guitar's] faults . . . lie in whoever plays it, and not in the guitar itself, for I have seen some people accomplish things on one string for which others would need the range of an organ. Everyone must make of it what he can, good or bad."

The Napoleonic war, at the turn of the nineteenth century, was responsible for repopularizing the guitar. The war, which carried on throughout Europe, reintroduced Europeans to the guitar-based music of Spain. This period led to the work of such composers and performers as Fernando Sor, Mauro Guilliani, Matteo Carcassi, and Ferdinando Carulli.

The first modern concerto for guitar and orchestra, Concerto No. 1 in A Major, was composed and performed by the Italian virtuoso Mauro

Guilliani. Among other things, it uses the right-hand thumb for bass notes, and it has a strong orchestral structure, with variations on a theme, a slow second movement, and finally a lively third movement.

Classical Guitar

Two people are responsible for the classical guitar as we know it today. The first was the brilliant guitar maker Antonio Torres. Torres revolutionized the building of a guitar, making a careful study of how it made its sound, where it came from, and how he could improve it. The other was the Spanish virtuoso Francisco Tarrega.

The Torres guitar, developed between the 1850s and the 1890s, had more volume than previous designs. It included a larger, deeper body and an aesthetically pleasing shape that is familiar today. Torres was the first maker to use "fan" bracing underneath the top. He once built a guitar with a spruce top and papier-mâché back and sides to prove his theory that it was the top that produced most of the volume.

Tarrega adopted the newly designed instrument, and composed and arranged hundreds of pieces for it. Ironically, Tarrega did not perform in public much. He was, however, an influential teacher, with a close circle of students and friends who acted almost like disciples in the world outside Tarrega's home and studio.

And then, at the dawn of the twentieth century, there arrived a young self-taught musician named Andrés Segovia. Before Segovia, people believed it was not possible for a solo guitarist to perform effectively to a large audience in a concert hall. Since Segovia, the world has become filled with guitarists in concert. In 1924, he made his debuts in London and Paris. He performed, transcribed, taught, and discovered a tremendous amount of music for the guitar. He also encouraged many composers to write for the instrument. He managed to reawaken interest in J. S. Bach, and arranged many Bach pieces for the guitar, which he performed and recorded.

Of Segovia's many gifts to the world, perhaps his most lasting was to make the guitar *the* popular instrument of the twentieth century. He also standardized the way guitar fingering is notated on scores (by showing the string number written within a circle over a series of notes that could be played elsewhere on the instrument), and settled the debate among classical guitarists about nails versus fingertips (by popularizing the use of plucking the strings with the nails of the right hand). By traveling and performing throughout the world, he brought respect and recognition to the instrument and left behind a vast body of work and pupils who have gone on to become maestros in their own right.

Flamenco

There are many different styles of playing, and while the guitar was gaining legitimacy in concert halls, a parallel evolution was taking place in the bars and cafés of nineteenth-century Spain. Flamenco has three aspects: singing, dancing, and guitar playing. It grew from the melding of Spanish folk cultures and the Middle Eastern influence of seven centuries of Moorish and Arabic occupation, particularly in Andalucia, in the north of Spain, where a large population of gypsies lived.

The Heartbeat of Spain

It was the Andalucian gypsies who turned flamenco into the heartbeat of Spain, although its roots are probably in Roman-occupied Spain. The composers Kodaly and Bartok discovered in their research into folk tunes that beautiful folksongs have a way of ending up as "beggars' songs." In the same way, the outcasts of Spain—the gypsies—adopted and preserved the musical traditions of the Moorish Arabs who had once ruled the land.

What remained, and became idiosyncratically gypsy, were the traditions of whip-cracking dance rhythms, and the troubadour's ability to improvise, composing verses about anything and everything at the drop of a hat. In the underground jargon of eighteenth-century Andalucia, someone *flamenco* was a dazzler, a "dude with attitude." And the music came to be popularized by performers considered by many to be the haughtiest and most flamboyant of the gypsies.

Spain is a dancing country, and the simplest nineteenth-century village dance orchestra might consist of a guitar and a tambourine, with dancers wielding castanets. By the 1850s and beyond, it was also a country at war with itself; but whether royalist or revolutionary, the tradition was never to shoot a man with a guitar—at least until he was given a chance to play, anyway.

Flamenco on the Move

The rhythmic and melodic early forms called *seguidilla* and *rasgueado* developed new and exciting forms in the café cantantes, bars with areas for performers. Gradually, guitar players developed short instrumental melodic interludes with variations, called *falsetas*.

What had for centuries been campfire entertainment suddenly found itself on a stage attracting the attention and applause of Europe's leading writers, poets, painters, and musicians—including Chopin, Liszt, George Sand, Alexandre Dumas, Edouard Manet, and Jules Verne—who discovered the joys and inexpensive excitement of Spain on their "grand vacations."

FACTS

The flamenco guitar sounds different from the classical guitar because cypress wood is used for the back and sides, instead of rosewood. The use of the capo (a clamp that goes around the neck and shortens the string length) also affects the tone, giving the strings a more treble sound.

Ramon Montoya is considered the father of modern flamenco guitar. Before his passing in 1949, he pioneered the recording of the style and developed its traditions and techniques. In doing so, he enriched the music's vocabulary and established himself as one of the first flamenco virtuosos of the twentieth century.

His real contribution, however, was to be the first person to break free of the role of accompanist and become established as a solo instrumentalist. When he performed in concert in Paris in 1936, he met with great acclaim.

It has been said that as flamenco has moved from the cafés to the nightclubs, the players have become more circuslike in the manner in which they play the guitar—wearing gloves, putting the instrument behind their heads, anything to attract and hold an audience's attention. Nevertheless, the twentieth century has produced some stunning players, such as Sabicas, Carlos Montoya, Nino Ricardo, Paco de Lucia, and Paco Pena.

The Electric Guitar
Early Development

The European troubadour traditions of folk music, and the spiritual music of African slaves, evolved into a guitar- and banjo-based music that in time became ragtime and then jazz. The guitar's role was problematic, though, because it never seemed loud enough to cut through all the other instruments of the group. That was one reason for the banjo's popularity—it might not be as sophisticated a musical instrument as the guitar, but in an ensemble situation it held its own against a blaring cornet, braying trombone, squawking clarinet, and the thumping of a drummer and the crash of his cymbals.

The concept of using the guitar like a trumpet or saxophone to play melodic solos began with the brilliant blues and jazz guitarist Lonnie Johnson. If you listen to his recordings with Louis Armstrong in the mid-1920s, you can hear the two young virtuosos create a musical art form—jazz—in their Hot Five and Hot Seven record dates. Johnson followed this up with a series of terrific jazz guitar duo recordings (the first that are known) with another guitar virtuoso, Eddie Lang.

FACTS

The development of the guitar had moved from the old world to the new when the German Christian Martin established the Martin guitar manufacturing company in New York in 1833. The guitars he made were different from those of the Spanish; they were bigger and used steel strings instead of sheep gut.

In France in the late 1920s and 1930s, the gypsy outsider Django Reinhardt took Lonnie Johnson's single-note concept—he was no doubt also influenced by Eddie Lang's classic early recordings with the violinist Joe Venuti—and developed it using a revolutionary new guitar, the Selmer Maccaférri. This design had an enlarged body, a D-shaped sound hole, and special internal strutting that made the instrument far louder than conventional guitars. What's more, Django was a near-genius on the instrument and played it with a fiery, inventive style that is still breathtaking to listen to.

More Volume

The search for more volume led Lloyd Loar, an engineer at the Gibson guitar company, to play around with electrified guitars and amplifiers. In 1924, his experiments with magnetic coils led to the development of a basic pickup, which was, in effect, a giant magnet shaped like a horseshoe that acted as a microphone for each of the strings of the guitar. The signal was then fed through a speaker with a volume control and a tone control. It was all very rudimentary stuff. Gibson didn't get the idea, though, and Loar left and formed the Vivitone company, which produced commercial guitar pickups during the 1930s.

The First Commercial Electric Guitar

The real breakthrough came in 1931, when Paul Barth and George Beauchamp joined forces with Adolph Rickenbacker to form the Electro String Company. They then produced the first commercially available electric guitar, the A22 and A25 cast-aluminum lap-steel guitar, known as the "frying pan" because of its shape.

Strictly speaking, the "frying pan" wasn't really an electric version of a traditional guitar, rather that of a lap-steel or Hawaiian guitar. However, in 1932 they produced the Electro Spanish, which was an archtop, or F-hole, steel-string guitar fitted with a horseshoe magnet. Gibson finally caught on, and adapted their L-50 archtop model into the now famous ES-150 electric model, which first appeared in 1936.

The musician who was to make the electric guitar a household word, Charlie Christian, was not actually the first electric guitar player. That role fell to Eddie Durham, who played a resonator guitar in Bennie Moten's jazz group from 1929 and recorded the first electric guitar solo, "Hittin' the Bottle," in 1935, with Jimmie Lunceford's band. He then made some historic recordings in New York City in 1937 and 1938 with the Kansas City Six, a spinoff group of musicians from Count Basie's Big Band that featured Lester Young on clarinet as well as saxophone. For the first time, the guitar was easily a match in volume and single-note improvisation for the saxophone and clarinet of Lester Young, and the trumpet of Buck Clayton.

There was one fundamental problem with the electric guitar, though—it kept feeding back. The amplified sound from the speaker would cause the body of the guitar to vibrate until a howl started that could only be stopped by turning the volume off. Guitarists found they were continually adjusting their volume levels to stop their instruments from feeding back. The answer was to create an instrument that didn't vibrate in sympathy with its amplified sound.

The Solid-Bodied Guitar

There's no definitive agreement about who produced the first solid-bodied guitar. Guitarist Les Paul created a "Log" guitar, using a Gibson neck on a flat piece of wood. He went to Gibson to get it into production, but Gibson, once again, was not impressed and turned him down.

At the same time, country guitarist Merle Travis was working with engineer Paul Bigsby, and they produced about a dozen solid-body guitar prototypes. However, the man who made the first commercially available solid-body guitar was Leo Fender, the owner of an electrical repair shop. In 1946 he founded the Fender Electrical Instrument Company to produce Hawaiian guitars and amplifiers. Encouraged by an employee, George Fullerton, they designed and eventually marketed a line of solid-body guitars called the Fender Broadcaster in 1950. The Gretsch drum company manufactured drums called Broadcaster, however, and told Fender he couldn't use that name. So Fender changed the name of his guitar to the Telecaster. The rest is history.

The solid-bodied electric guitar paved the way for the popularization of urban blues and an R&B boom in the 1950s, with such great musicians as Howlin' Wolf, Muddy Waters, B. B. King, and so forth. These musicians in turn influenced a generation of young rock-and-roll players in the 1960s in England, including Eric Clapton, Jeff Beck, Robert Fripp, and Jimmy Page.

And Beyond . . .

Perhaps the most revolutionary advance of the last twenty years has been the development of MIDI, or Musical Instrument Digital Interface, a computer protocol that allows computers, synthesizers, and other equipment to talk to each other. While electronic music has been primarily a computer and keyboard-oriented process, the guitar synthesizer is coming into its own. In the past it has had some problems with delay and tracking (how quickly, in effect, you can play one note after the other), but that seems to be disappearing with each new generation of equipment.

An example of the new guitar is the SynthAxe, developed in England in 1984. This guitar synthesizer is played via an innovative fretboard touch system. The neck acts as a MIDI controller, allowing the player to produce a full range of synthesized and sampled sounds.

Other guitarists have experimented with adding extra strings to the existing six, ranging from seven to forty-two or more. But one thing seems constant: All of the players of the experimental guitars end up continuing to use the traditional, simple six-string guitar regardless of what else they play.

Where we go from here is anyone's guess—but one thing is for sure: Somewhere in the background is likely to be the twang and strum of a simple six-string guitar.

History of the Guitar at a Glance

1700 B.C.   Rumor has it that Hermes, the Greek messenger of the gods, invents the seven-string lyre, the forerunner of the guitar. Meanwhile, at about the same time in Egypt, pictures of a guitarlike instrument are being painted on the walls of tombs.

500 B.C.   The *cithara* develops from the lyre.

1265   Juan Gil of Zamora mentions the early guitar in *Ars Musica*.

1283–1350   *Guitarra latina* and *Guitar moresca* are mentioned multiple times in the poems of the Archpriest of Hita.

1306   A "gitarer" was played at the Feast of Westminster in England.

1381   Three Englishmen are sent to prison for making a disturbance with "giternes."

1404   *Der mynnen regein* by Eberhard Von Cersne makes reference to a "quinterne."

1487   Johannes Tinctoris described the *guitarra* as being invented by the Catalans.

1535   "El Maestro," by Luis Milan, is published, and contains the earliest known *vihuela* music, including courtly dances known as *pavanes*.

1551–1555   Nine books of tablature are published by Adrian Le Roy. These include the first pieces for five-course guitar. The addition of the fifth course was attributed to Vicente Espinel.

1674   The *Guitarre Royal,* by Francesco Corbetta, is published. Dedicated to Louis XIV of France, it increases the guitar's popularity.

1770–1800	The five courses (doubled strings) are replaced by single strings, and a sixth string is added to the guitar.
1800–1850	Fernando Sor, Mauro Guilliani, Matteo Carcassi, and Dionisio Aguado all perform, teach, write, and publish their compositions. The guitar begins to enjoy wide popularity.
1833	Christian Frederick Martin arrives in New York City and founds the Martin guitar manufacturing company.
1850–1892	Guitar maker Antonio Torres develops the larger, more resonant instrument we know today.
1902	The Gibson Mandolin-Guitar Manufacturing Company is founded in Kalamazoo, Michigan, and quickly becomes one of the most famous guitar manufacturers in the world.
1916	Segovia performs at Ateneo, the most important concert hall in Madrid. Previously, it was thought that the guitar did not have the volume for this type of venue.
1931	The Electro String Company is founded, and the A22 and A25 cast-aluminum lap-steel guitars, known as "frying pans" because of their shape, become the first commercially produced electric guitars.
1950	The Fender Solid Body Telecaster first appears.
1960	The guitar is finally accepted as a serious musical instrument for study at the Royal College of Music in London.
1960s	Jimi Hendrix falls off stage by mistake and breaks his guitar trying to throw it back on stage. It becomes part of his stage act and starts a trend.
1984	The SynthAxe makes its appearance in England.

CHAPTER 2

Famous Classical and Flamenco Guitarists

Andrés Segovia (1893–1987)

Many musicians feel that without Segovia's efforts, the guitar would still be considered the equivalent of a "honky tonk" barroom instrument. He is considered the father of the modern classical guitar.

He was born in Linares, Spain, in 1893. When he was four years old, his uncle used to sing songs to him and pretend to strum an imaginary guitar. A local *luthier* (guitar maker) made an instrument for the child, and although Segovia was actively discouraged by his family, he single-mindedly pursued his studies of the instrument. While self-taught, he adopted many of the techniques and practices of Francisco Tarrega, the influential late-nineteenth-century guitar maestro.

In 1909 he made his debut at the age of sixteen in Grenada at the Centro Artistico, and he performed his professional debut in Madrid in 1912. It was met with disbelief by many because the guitar was widely believed to be incapable of proper classical expression, but Segovia stunned his critics with his skill. From 1916 he toured South America, and in 1924 he debuted in both London and Paris, becoming known as the "ambassador of the guitar." He made his American debut in New York City in 1928. He had a wide repertoire of lyrical works, which he played with great emotional expressiveness using fingernails on gut strings. He also demanded silence and concentration from his audiences.

The Messenger

As Segovia grew older, he came to consider himself the messenger who would bring the guitar to the world concert stage so that it could take its place beside the violin and the piano. Before long, composers like Heitor Villa-Lobos began to compose original pieces specifically for the guitar. Segovia himself arranged many pieces from the classical canon for the guitar—most notably by J. S. Bach, whom he resurrected from the shadows of the musical canon and turned into a popular twentieth-century composer—as well as lute and harpsichord music.

The central problem Segovia faced during his early career was making sure the guitar's sound would fill a concert hall. Over the years, Segovia solved the dilemma by experimenting with playing guitars made with new woods and designs, all to increase the instrument's natural amplification. During the 1940s, he adopted nylon for his strings rather than gut, and started a practice that continues to this day. The development of nylon strings gave the guitar more consistent tones, while projecting the sound much farther and being much less likely to break.

He also standardized the way guitar fingering is notated on scores (by showing the string number written within a circle over a series of notes that could be played elsewhere on the instrument), and settled the debate among classical guitarists about nails versus fingertips (by popularizing the use of plucking the strings with the nails of the right hand).

FACTS

Segovia played a Ramirez classical guitar from 1912 until the 1930s, when he met the German *luthier* (guitar maker) Hermann Hauser. Hauser was so impressed with Segovia's guitar that he changed the way he built guitars, and presented Segovia with a new instrument in 1937 that the maestro used until the 1960s.

Segovia's Gift

Of Segovia's many gifts to the world, perhaps his most lasting was to make the guitar *the* popular instrument of the twentieth century. In addition to recording and performing, Segovia spent the remainder of his life and career successfully influencing the authorities at conservatories, academies, and universities to include the guitar in their instruction programs with the same emphasis given the violin, cello, and piano. He continued to give concerts into his eighties. His early struggles are recounted in his 1983 memoir, *Andrés Segovia: An Autobiography of the Years 1893–1920*. He died in 1987.

Julian Bream (1933–)

Born in London in 1933, Bream is considered by many students of classical music as the premier guitar and lute virtuoso of the twentieth century. He was an admirer of the Belgian gypsy jazz musician Django

Reinhardt, and began his musical career playing a steel-string guitar. When he heard a recording of Segovia playing "Recuerdos de la Alhambra," he was captivated and devoted his time to studying the classical guitar.

FACTS

American Sharon Isbin was the first person to be appointed Professor of Guitar at Julliard Music School in New York in 1989.

He was largely self-taught (although helped by the Philharmonic Society of Guitarists), and he attended the Royal College of Music. There he studied piano and composition, because the guitar was not considered a "serious" instrument at that time.

His public debut was at the Cheltenham Art Gallery in England in 1946, and he began broadcasting for BBC Radio in the late 1940s. He also took up the lute and studied and played early music. In 1960 he founded the Julian Bream Consort, an ensemble of original instrument virtuosi that enjoyed astounding success, greatly revitalizing interest in the music of the Elizabethan era.

By the 1950s he had won fame for his technique and mastery of a wide range of musical styles. Like Segovia, he encouraged composers to write for the guitar, but unlike Segovia, Bream encouraged fresh, sometimes dissonant, modern material, which he nevertheless managed to perform with a striking tone and great emotionality.

Christopher Parkening (1947–)

One of the premiere classical guitarists for the past twenty-five years, Parkening has received three Grammy nominations for best classical performance and holds an honorary doctorate in music from Montana State University, where he teaches a master class each summer. Parkening continues to inspire and awe audiences around the world with both his technical brilliance and musicianship, performing more than eighty concerts a year.

John Williams (1941–)

Born in Australia, Williams began learning the guitar at the age of four at the knee of his father, Len, who was also a gifted guitarist. When the family moved to London in 1952, he met and studied with Segovia, and on his recommendation entered the Accademia Musicale di Siena in Italy, where he won a scholarship to study and stayed until 1961.

In 1958, at the request of his fellow students, he was the first student, of any instrument, to give a complete solo recital at the Accademia Musicale. He began recording and touring, and in 1960 he was made Professor of Guitar at the Royal College of Music in London.

Williams was dubbed by Segovia "the prince of the guitar," and his brilliant technique soon attracted worldwide attention. He and Bream played and recorded a series of duets and recorded works as diverse as transcriptions of Scarlatti and Andre Previn's "Guitar Concerto."

While the older Bream encouraged contemporary composers to write for the instrument, he was also instrumental in a revitalization of early music. Williams, on the other hand, has been in the forefront of breaking down the barriers between classical music and popular music. He has performed with flamenco guitarists, and at Ronnie Scott's Jazz Club in London, as well as in rock concerts playing steel-strung acoustic and electric instruments. His album *Changes* (1971) features arrangements of songs by the Beatles and Joni Mitchell, as well as a rock version of J. S. Bach's Prelude from the Suite in E Major. The piece "Cavatina" actually hit the popular charts in England briefly. In 1979 he formed Sky, a group that fused classical, jazz, and pop ideas.

FACTS

Ida Presti and Alexandre Lagoya were the first well-known twentieth-century classical guitar duo. Presti had the unusual technique of using the sides, rather than the tips, of her fingernails.

Narcisco Yepes (1927–1997)

Yepes was a Spanish guitarist of agility, precision, and execution. He was the first to commercially record Rodrigo's "Concerto de Aranjuez" in 1955. In the early 1960s he began to play a ten-string classical guitar to which he had added four bass strings tuned to C, B-flat, A-flat, and G-flat. These extra strings helped him arrange and play the piano compositions of composers such as Albeniz and Falla on the guitar, as well as fuller transcriptions of baroque music by composers such as Teleman and Scarlatti.

The "Concerto de Aranjuez" (1939) is one of the most famous pieces of music written for guitar and orchestra. It was written by the blind Spanish composer Joaquin Rodrigo.

Ramon Montoya (1880–1949)

Born into a flamenco-playing gypsy family, he was influenced by Rafael Marin, who had studied with the great classical guitar master Francisco Tarrega. Montoya's playing was sophisticated and built on traditions, while adding new ideas and enriching the flamenco vocabulary. Early in his career in the 1920s, he accompanied many of the major singers and dancers in the Café de La Marina in Madrid and won renown as a virtuoso player.

His most important contribution to flamenco, however, was to break free of the role of accompanist and become a solo instrumentalist. He recorded many flamenco records, but his early recordings, such as "Granadina," made in Paris in the 1930s, are among some of the most exciting and extraordinary.

Flamenco guitars have a different sound than classical guitars, due to lighter construction, cypress wood bodies, and lower string action.

Carlos Montoya (1903–1993)

Like his uncle Ramon Montoya, Carlos also became a successful and influential flamenco guitarist.

Born into a gypsy family in Spain, his interest in music and the guitar began at an early age. He began studying the guitar with his mother and a neighboring barber, eventually learning from Pepe el Barbero, a guitarist and teacher.

Carlos started playing professionally at the age of fourteen, accompanying singers and dancers at the cafés in Madrid. Two of the dancers he most often played for were La Teresina and La Argentina.

From the 1920s he began touring Europe, Asia, and North America. At the time World War II broke out in 1939, Carlos was on tour with a dancer in the United States. He decided to settle in New York City, eventually becoming a United States citizen. By the end of the war, Carlos had opened his repertoire to include not only flamenco, but also blues, jazz, and folk music. He became the first flamenco guitarist to tour the world with symphonies and orchestras. He performed on television and recorded more than forty albums, including "Suite Flamenco," a concerto he performed with the St. Louis Symphony Orchestra in 1966.

Carlos Montoya transformed flamenco from a dance accompaniment to a serious form of guitar music with a style all its own. With his own style, he adapted it to other genres of music, all along making himself an international star. He died at the age of eighty-nine in Wainscott, New York.

Sabicas (1912–1990)

His real name was Agustin Castellon Campos, and he was born of a gypsy family in the north of Spain. A prodigy whose virtuoso style helped define modern flamenco, he left Spain in 1937 for Mexico, where he formed a company with the flamenco dancer Carmen Amaya that toured the world, making recordings.

By the mid-1950s, Sabicas moved to New York, where he concentrated on a solo career as a concert and recording artist. His dramatic style, and breathtakingly accurate articulation and technique, became a blueprint for succeeding generations of flamenco players. A powerful improviser, he once said he could never play the same thing twice.

Paco de Lucia (1947–)

One of the leading flamenco guitarists of the late twentieth century, Paco de Lucia was born in Algeciras, in the south of Spain, into a family of talented flamenco players. He began playing at the age of seven. Not only did his father encourage him to spend hours practicing, but his house was sometimes visited by Nino Ricardo, a major flamenco guitarist who had studied and played with Ramon Montoya. de Lucia later discovered the recordings of Sabicas, whose speed and clean execution had a profound influence on the development of his style.

At fourteen, he won first prize in a major flamenco competition. In 1962, he accompanied the singing of his brother Pepe, and the two of them won the top prizes at the Jerez Concurso, a prestigious music festival. The following year he joined Jose Greco's dance troupe and toured the United States, meeting Sabicas and others.

He was greatly inspired by a trip to Brazil, and began a series of innovative developments in flamenco guitar style, based on new rhythms derived from Brazilian music and jazz. In addition to leading his own sextet, de Lucia enjoyed a long and creative partnership with leading flamenco singer, El Camaron de la Isla.

Increasingly influenced by jazz, by the end of the 1970s he was working with John McLaughlin, and Larry Coryell, and then in the 1980s he and McLaughlin went on to work with Al DiMeola.

In 1991, he memorized and recorded Rodrigo's famous "Concerto de Aranjuez," which he played with a flamenco feel. The release of 1999's *Luzia* heralded de Lucia's return to traditional flamenco, though he continues to play in other music forms with other musicians.

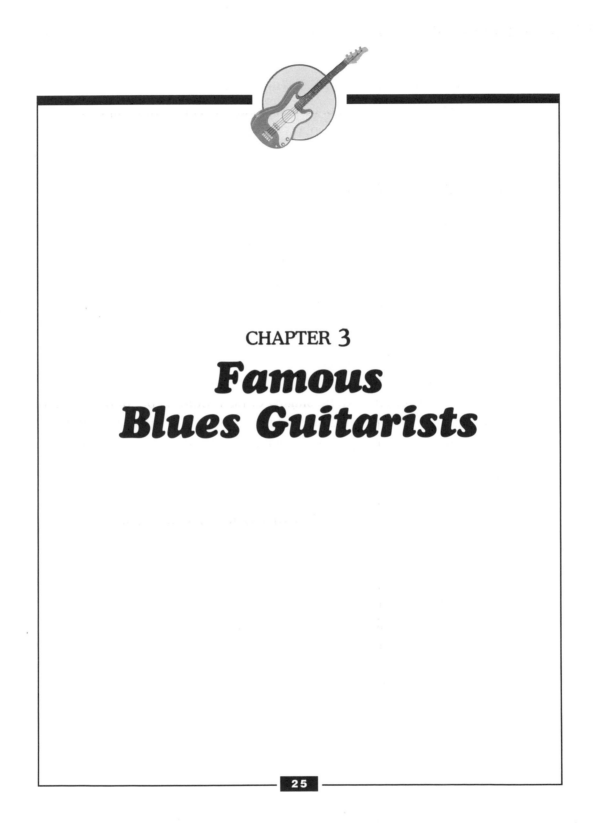

CHAPTER 3

Famous
Blues Guitarists

Charley Patton (1887–1934)

Born in Mississippi, Patton was considered one of the early innovative and influential figures in blues, ragtime, country songs, and spirituals. His "Pony Blues," recorded in 1929, became a commercial success that made him a star in blues circles. He played with a loose style that bent bar lengths and timing, though his style was nevertheless earthy and rhythmic.

FACTS

Charley Patton was one of the great blues showmen. He played often at "jukes" (small bars), and often on street corners. One of his tricks, later adopted by rock musicians such as Jimi Hendrix, was to play the guitar behind his back.

With careful listening, you can hear him play instrumental responses to his sung phrases. He evoked sounds from the guitar, in a crude percussive style, snapping strings and drumming on the instrument. He also tuned his guitar higher than normal to give it a bright, penetrating sound. By the time of his death in 1934, he had become a legendary figure in the Mississippi Delta who had influenced countless other blues musicians.

Big Bill Broonzy (1893–1958)

Born in Scott, Mississippi, to a sharecropping family, Broonzy learned the rudiments of the fiddle before his family moved to Arkansas. By the age of fourteen, he was working for tips at country dances and picnics. Sometime in the early 1920s he moved to Chicago, where, under the guidance of Papa Charlie Jackson, he learned to play blues guitar. Big Bill Broonzy's brand of blues stretched from ragtime-influenced blues to city blues backed with jazz musicians, and to traditional folk blues and spirituals. He is considered the godfather of the Chicago blues scene.

Broonzy influenced many young bluesmen, and often took artists of lesser stature under his wing, helping them secure recording sessions and performance dates. His stature as a blues artist grew far beyond the Chicago scene after his performances at John Hammond's famous

Spirituals to Swing concert series in 1938 and 1939 at Carnegie Hall in New York City.

In 1951 he toured Europe, helping to introduce blues to France and England and opening the door for other American blues artists. In 1955, with help from writer Yannick Bruynoghe, he wrote his autobiography, *Big Bill's Blues*. Originally published in London, the book was one of the earliest autobiographies by a bluesman. Two years later, he was diagnosed with throat cancer. He continued to perform, often in great pain, and he died of the disease in 1958. He was inducted into the Blues Foundation's Hall of Fame in 1980.

Blind Lemon Jefferson (1897–1929)

Considering he was the most popular male blues recording artist of the 1920s, little is known about Blind Lemon Jefferson. He was born in Couchman, near Wortham, in Freestone County, Texas, in 1897. He was blind from childhood, possibly even from birth. Between 1925 and 1929, he made at least 100 recordings, including alternate versions of some songs, and issued forty-three records.

He had few imitators, due to the technical complexity of his guitar playing and the distinctiveness of his high, clear voice. As a young man, Jefferson took up the guitar and became a street musician, playing in Wortham and nearby East Texas towns such as Groesbeck (mentioned in his "Penitentiary Blues"), Buffalo, and Marlin. Around 1917 he moved to Dallas, playing in the area centered on Deep Ellum, Dallas's equivalent of Memphis's Beale Street.

It was here that he met up with Leadbelly, an older and more experienced musician with a large repertoire of songs. Nonetheless, it was the younger man who had the greater command of the blues. They played together in Dallas until Leadbelly was sentenced to go to prison for assault.

FACTS

Blind Lemon Jefferson played a Stella guitar, developed from twelve-string guitars (made up of six pairs of strings, with some strings tuned in unison and others an octave apart), which were common in Central and South America.

In the early 1920s, Jefferson played around the South, especially the Mississippi Delta region, where there was lucrative work for an itinerant bluesman. He sold more than a million "race records" to the emergent African-American market during the 1920s, but nevertheless died a pauper in Chicago, in mysterious circumstances, toward the end of December 1929.

Leadbelly (1885–1945)

Huddie William Ledbetter was born on Jeter Plantation in Mooringsport, Louisiana, in 1885 into a relatively prosperous family, who farmed land first as sharecroppers in Louisiana, then as landowners on the Texas-Louisiana border. Taught to play accordion and then guitar by his uncle Terrel Ledbetter, he soon blossomed and began to employ his talents at local "sukey-jump" parties and down on Shreveport's notorious Fannin Street.

After fathering a second child at age sixteen, Leadbelly, propelled by an outraged community, left home to become an itinerant minstrel and a farm laborer. He roamed around Dallas with the legendary blues singer Blind Lemon Jefferson, though they parted company in 1917, when Leadbelly was jailed for assault. This was the first of many years spent in Southern penitentiaries.

He got his nickname, Leadbelly, in prison because of his physical toughness. He escaped from prison and returned home, but after hiding out briefly on the farm, he went to New Orleans and lived under the assumed name Walter Boyd. However, he got into a fight with a relative, Will Stafford, and Stafford was shot in the head and killed. Though Leadbelly always maintained his innocence, he was convicted of murder and assault to kill, and sentenced as Walter Boyd to a long term of hard labor on the Shaw State Farm.

His musical gifts served him well in the prison camps, where he became a favorite of the guards. Legend has it that in 1925 Leadbelly pleaded for (and was given) his release in a "please pardon me" song composed for and addressed to Governor Neff. After receiving Neff's pardon, Leadbelly returned to Mooringsport, Louisiana, but his womanizing and rough ways led to yet another conviction for assault with intent to murder. In the Louisiana state prison farm at Angola, the authorities discovered his previous conviction and considered this an aggravating factor. They turned down his written pleas for an early release. Records show he was flogged severely for relatively minor incidents.

Discovery

In the 1930s, the Texas folklorist John Lomax was traveling through the South under a Library of Congress grant, among other things recording the "musical treasury locked up" in the prisons. Lomax discovered Leadbelly at Angola in July 1933. He was astounded by Leadbelly's enormous repertoire, intense vocal style, and commanding physical presence. Using state-of-the-art equipment for the day, a bulky recorder that cut aluminum discs and occupied most of the trunk of his car, Lomax began recording Leadbelly.

Under "double good time" measures adopted to save costs, Leadbelly was released early from prison. Lomax decided to take Leadbelly to New York. There, he performed before audiences of musicologists at elite universities, inspiring fear and admiration. The mystique of his convict past and his commanding physical presence, replete with horrific scars, added to his allure. His eclectic repertoire, performed on a twelve-string guitar—which was not widely used then—was largely unknown, and harked back some thirty or more years to near-forgotten rural traditions. John Lomax also negotiated a contract with Macmillan publishers to write a book that would be titled *Negro Folk Songs as Sung by Leadbelly*. It detailed Leadbelly's history and the events surrounding his discovery by Lomax, together with transcripts from his repertoire and explanations about the background of his songs and their place in American folklore.

Lomax also arranged a recording contract with the American Record Company, which had highly sophisticated recording studios and equipment. However, the commercial success of rural blues had passed some ten years earlier, with the heyday of Blind Lemon Jefferson, and the records sold poorly. This was compounded by the company's insistence that he record blues rather than the folksongs that dominated his repertoire, most of which predated the blues and were the chief source of his attraction for white audiences. As the stay in New York and environs wore on, the relationship between Lomax and Leadbelly deteriorated, and they parted company in March of 1935.

Survival Instinct

Leadbelly survived on odd jobs and welfare. The Lomax book was now in print and gained him some publicity, despite its poor sales. The African-American music market had moved on, and Leadbelly continued to find his principal audience among whites, especially the trade union movement and its left-wing associates. Always ready to adapt to his environment, Leadbelly added topical and protest songs to his repertoire for the first time, tackling segregation and other issues.

In early 1939 he was arrested yet again, for assaulting a black man with a knife, and he eventually served eight months on Rykers Island. In early 1940, at the age of fifty-one, Leadbelly was released. Moving back into the New York folk circuit, he met up with newcomers Woody Guthrie, Sonny Terry, Brownie McGhee, Pete Seeger, The Golden Gate Quartet, Burl Ives, and many others who had migrated to New York and would fuel a minor folk boom during and after the second world war.

He came to resent the "convict" image that he had acquired, but found it impossible to shake off. He toured briefly in France, where jazz had become hugely popular, in early 1949. While in Paris, persistent muscle problems led to a diagnosis of Lou Gehrig's disease, amyotrophic lateral sclerosis. Six months later, on December 6, 1949, he died. In 1950, his trademark song, "Goodnight Irene," became a nationwide Number 1 hit for the Weavers.

FACTS

The Gibson 335 guitar, a symmetrical, thin-bodied instrument that became the mainstay for bluesmen such as B. B. King and Freddie King, first appeared in 1958.

Howlin' Wolf (1910–1975)

Born Chester Arthur Burnett, this man's musical influence extends from the rockabilly singers of the 1950s and the classic rock stars of the 1960s to the grunge groups of the 1990s, plus a legion of imitators to rival Elvis.

Born on June 10, 1910, in White Station, Mississippi, a tiny railroad stop between Aberdeen and West Point in the Mississippi hill country, Chester was fascinated by music as a boy and would often beat on pans with a stick and imitate the whistle of the railroad trains that ran nearby. He also sang in the choir at the White Station Baptist Church, where Will Young, his stern, unforgiving uncle, preached.

When his parents separated, his father moved to the Delta, and his mother left Chester with his uncle Will, who treated him harshly. His mother spent much of her adult life as a street singer, eking out a living selling handwritten gospel songs for pennies to passersby. She disowned her son, claiming he played "the Devil's music." Chester's paranoid rants about women in some of his songs can be traced to this bleak mother-son relationship.

Becoming a Wolf

When he was thirteen, Chester ran away to rejoin his father and half-siblings, who lived on the Young and Morrow Plantation near Ruleville. There, Chester became fascinated by local blues musicians, especially the Delta's first great blues star, Charlie Patton, who lived on the nearby Dockery Plantation.

When his father bought Chester his first guitar in January 1928, he also convinced Patton to give Chester guitar lessons. Chester later took impromptu harmonica lessons from Sonny Boy Williamson, who was romancing his half-sister, Mary. He learned to sing by listening to the records of musicians like Blind Lemon Jefferson, Jimmie "the Singing Brakeman" Rodgers, and Lonnie Johnson. When he wasn't working on his father's farm, he traveled the Delta with musicians such as Robert Johnson, Charlie Patton, Son House, and Willie Brown, playing guitar and blues harp simultaneously, using a rack-mounted harp. From the start,

Chester's voice was so huge and raw, like Charley Patton's, that he earned the nickname Howlin' Wolf.

Rising to Fame

In 1948, at age 38, he moved to West Memphis, Arkansas, where he put together a band that included harmonica players James Cotton and Junior Parker, and guitarists Pat Hare, Matt "Guitar" Murphy, and Willie Johnson. He also got a spot on radio station KWEM, playing blues and endorsing farm gear. In 1951, Wolf came to the attention of a young but very influential Memphis record producer, Sam Phillips, who took him into the studio and recorded "Moanin' at Midnight" and "How Many More Years," and leased them to Chess Records. Released in 1952, they made it to the Top 10 on Billboard's R&B charts. Wolf then moved to Chicago in 1953 and called the city home for the rest of his life. Phillips, who also discovered Elvis Presley, Carl Perkins, Jerry Lee Lewis, Johnny Cash, and Charlie Rich, said that losing Wolf to Chicago was his biggest career disappointment.

In his later years, Wolf continued to perform with a manic intensity, often in small clubs that other well-known bluesmen had already abandoned. He played electric guitar with his bare fingers—an oddity for a Chicago bluesman—and his eccentric, slashing style made him a favorite guitarist of Eric Clapton, Jimmy Page, Stevie Ray Vaughan, and Jimi Hendrix.

The Last Performance

In the late 1960s, Wolf suffered several heart attacks, and in 1970 he was in an auto accident that destroyed his kidneys. For the rest of his life, he received dialysis treatments every three days. Despite his failing health, Howlin' Wolf stoically continued to record and perform.

In 1970, he recorded *The London Howlin' Wolf Sessions* in England with Eric Clapton, members of the Rolling Stones, and other British rock stars. It was his best-selling album, reaching Number 79 on the pop charts.

In 1973, he cut his last studio album, *Back Door Wolf*, which included the incendiary "Coon on the Moon," the autobiographical "Moving," and "Can't Stay Here," a tribute to Charley Patton. Wolf's last performance was in November 1975 at the Chicago Amphitheater. On a bill with B. B. King, Albert King, O. V. Wright, Luther Allison, and many other great bluesmen, Wolf almost literally rose from his deathbed to re-create many of his old songs, performing some of his old antics—such as crawling across the stage during the song "Crawling King Snake." The crowd went wild and gave him a five-minute standing ovation. He exerted himself so much that when he got offstage, a team of paramedics had to revive him. Two months later his heart gave out during an operation and he died.

He was inducted into the Blues Foundation's Hall of Fame in 1980 and the Rock & Roll Hall of Fame in 1991. His hometown of West Point, Mississippi, erected a statue in his honor in 1997, and continues to host a Howlin' Wolf music festival every summer.

Robert Johnson (1911–1938)

Robert Johnson was born May 8, 1911, in Hazlehurst, Mississippi, and moved with his mother to Robinsonville, a small but thriving northern Mississippi cotton community some twenty miles south of Memphis.

A consummate musician, his talent was so awe-inspiring that myths grew up around him, particularly one about selling his soul to the Devil at a crossroad at midnight in return for worldly success.

In his early teens, the harmonica was his main instrument for several years. He took up the guitar during the late 1920s. He made a rack for his harp out of baling wire and string and was soon picking out appropriate accompaniments for his harp and voice. Willie Brown, a musician of some renown and abilities, tried to show Johnson some things, and it was through Willie that Johnson met Charley Patton.

He farmed for a while, but both his sixteen-year-old wife, Virginia, and their baby died in childbirth in April 1930. Less than two months later, close to the first of June, Son House came to live in Robinsonville at the request of Willie Brown. House, a precarious combination of bluesman and preacher, brought with him an intensity in his music that was shared with no one, not even Patton. It was raw, direct emotion, and Johnson followed House and Brown wherever they went. Son House's influence can be clearly heard in Johnson's recordings of 1936 and 1937.

The country was deep in the Depression at that time, but central Mississippi was fortunate to have the federal government building highways in an attempt to provide work and an injection of cash into the economy. The Saturday night juke joints of the road gangs and lumber camps became Johnson's stage, and bluesman Ike Zinneman became his coach and mentor. Johnson also found out that women could provide almost everything else for him.

If he was going to be in any one place for a while, he developed a technique of female selection that generally kept him well fed and cared for. As soon as he hit town, he'd find a homely woman. A few kind words and he knew he'd have a warm smile and a place to stay anytime, though his womanizing more than once got him in a scrape.

He traveled up and down the river playing in levee camps, for road gangs, and in juke joints, visiting family and friends in Robinsonville and Memphis. He even roamed as far afield as Canada and New York in later years, but he always came home to Helena, Arkansas, one of the most musically active towns in the Delta.

All the great musicians of the era came through Helena. Sonny Boy Williamson, Robert Nighthawk, Honeyboy Edwards, Howlin' Wolf, and countless others performed in area night clubs and hot spots. Pretty soon the word would go out that Robert Johnson was going to be at such-and-such a place, and the people would come. They knew they'd have a good time and hear some fine music.

Johnson was protective about his guitar playing and was acutely aware of other musicians "ripping off" his "stuff." If someone was eyeing him too closely, he would get up in the middle of a song, make a feeble excuse, and disappear for months. It all seemed very quirky, although recent research has suggested that he may have been guarding a very personal method of tuning his guitar.

Out of necessity, he developed the ability to play almost anything requested of him. In addition to the blues for which he was known, he had a repertoire that included pop tunes, hillbilly tunes, polkas, square dances, sentimental songs, and ballads. Among the more common pieces he played were "Yes, Sir, That's My Baby," "My Blue Heaven," and "Tumbling Tumbleweeds."

It was said he could hear a piece just once and be able to play it. He could be deep in conversation with a group of people and hear something—never stop talking—and later be able to play it and sing it perfectly. It amazed some very fine musicians, and they never understood how he did it.

Enter Ernie

Ernie Oertle was the American Record Company salesman and informal talent scout for the mid-South in the late 1930s, and after an audition, Oertle decided to take Johnson to San Antonio, Texas, to record.

FACTS

Robert Johnson often played a Gibson L-1 with a pin bridge and a round (as opposed to F-shaped) sound hole. Gibson built its reputation on the archtops—or F holes—but began to introduce flat tops after 1926.

Johnson's first session in November 1936 yielded the song for which he is most widely remembered: "Terraplane Blues." It was his best seller and a fair-sized hit for Vocalion Records. He was invited back to Texas to cut some more sides the following June, but nothing sold as well as "Terraplane." Although six of Johnson's eleven records were still in the Vocalion catalog by December 1938, he wasn't called back that spring or even the following summer. Vocalion released one final 78 in February 1939, but that was probably due to a great deal of interest in him by John Hammond.

Johnson's Last Job

Sometime in August 1938, Johnson left Helena and swung through Robinsonville to see his people before playing a gig down in the Delta. As ever, he had become friends with a local woman—who unfortunately happened to be the wife of the man who ran the juke house at the intersection of Highways 82 and 49E, which the locals often referred to "Three Forks." It was here that Johnson played his last job.

On August 13, 1938, "Three Forks" offered the talents of Robert Johnson and singer and harmonica player Sonny Boy Williamson. There was a great deal of music and dancing that Saturday night, as both men sang and played their own brand of Delta blues.

Williamson noticed the attraction Johnson displayed for the lady of the house, as well as the marked tension in the room. He recognized a potentially explosive situation when he saw one.

During a break in the music, Johnson and Williamson were standing together when someone brought Johnson an open half-pint of whiskey. As he was about to drink from it, Williamson knocked it out of his hand, and it broke on the ground. He advised Johnson to never drink from an open bottle. But Johnson was angry and told Williamson to never knock whiskey out of his hand.

When a second open bottle was brought to Johnson, Williamson could do no more than stand by and watch. Back on the stand, it wasn't too long before Johnson could no longer sing. Williamson took up the slack for him with his voice and harmonica, but Johnson stopped short in the middle of a number and got up and went outside. Before the night was over he displayed definite signs of poisoning. It seems the houseman's jealousy finally got the best of him and he had laced Johnson's whisky with strychnine.

Ironically, Johnson survived the poisoning but contracted pneumonia. He died on Tuesday, August 16. He was twenty-seven years old.

He was buried in the graveyard of the Little Zion Church just north of Greenwood, Mississippi. Eleven 78 rpm records were issued during Johnson's lifetime and one posthumously. Including the material that never saw issuance on 78s, there are a total of forty-two recordings—the only recordings of one of the true geniuses of American music.

FACTS

Chicago Bluesman Otis Rush, who emerged in the 1950s, played guitar left-handed without reversing the strings, so the bass strings were at the top.

Lonnie Johnson (1899–1970)

Almost unique among twentieth-century musicians, Lonnie Johnson bestrides two of the most popular music forms of the early century—jazz and blues, defying categorization as belonging solely to either.

FACTS

Lonnie Johnson was a colossus who bestrode several genres of guitar, particularly blues and jazz. He often recorded using a Stella twelve-string, and a regular six-string archtop.

He helped define the guitar's role in blues playing, and his melodic ideas and jaunty singing were on a par only with jazz's first recorded genius, the trumpeter Louis Armstrong. It's perhaps no coincidence that he recorded in 1927 with Louis Armstrong's Hot Five. Armstrong may be considered the first jazz musician to step in front of a band and take an improvised solo, but Lonnie Johnson is the first guitarist to play a single-note improvised jazz chorus on the guitar. The two-guitar duets he recorded in 1928 and 1929 with jazz guitarist Eddie Lang—a musician who recorded several tracks for contractual reasons under the tongue-in-cheek name of Blind Willie Dunn—are groundbreaking in their inventiveness.

For more than forty years, Johnson played blues, jazz, and ballads, his versatility stemming in part from growing up in the musically diverse Crescent City, New Orleans. His first instrument was the violin, but he developed an unaccompanied style as a guitar player that was sophisticated, fluid, and melodic. He signed up with Okeh Records, and between 1925 and 1932 he cut an estimated 130 tracks.

He moved to Chicago and returned to recording in 1939. In 1947 he recorded one of his biggest hits, the ballad "Tomorrow Night," which topped the R&B charts for seven weeks in 1948. More hits followed, but by the late 1950s he was earning a living as a hotel janitor in Philadelphia.

He was "rediscovered" by banjo player Elmer Snowden, and enjoyed a major comeback, cutting a series of albums for Prestige's Bluesville subsidiary during the early 1960s. He also toured Europe with the American Folk Blues Festival.

Alas, in 1969, Johnson was hit by a car in Toronto and died a year later from the effects of the accident.

His influence was massive, from Robert Johnson, whose approach to guitar playing strongly resembled his older namesake, to Elvis Presley and Jerry Lee Lewis, each of whom at different times paid tribute with versions of "Tomorrow Night."

FACTS

Stevie Ray Vaughan played a Fender Stratocaster tuned down a semitone with heavy gage strings, few effects, and two amplifiers. His large sound and rhythmic improvisations have an almost acoustic quality to them.

B. B. King (1925-)

B. B. King and his musical "wife," his Gibson guitar "Lucille," is one of the most famous electric blues guitarists in the world. Inspired early on by Blind Lemon Jefferson and Lonnie Johnson, he also drew inspiration from early jazz guitarists such as Charlie Christian. He developed a style of playing that used the guitar not just as a rhythmic accompaniment, but also as a sort of "backup"—or accompanying voice—when he sang, playing short, riff-like single-note melodic phrases. His first hit came in 1951 with "3 O'clock Blues," and he went on to record many more, with big band accompaniment and jazzy phrasing.

FACTS

The Gibson ES-125 is basically a cheaper version of Gibson's first electric guitar production model, the ES-150. During the 1940s, B. B. King used a Fender Bassman amplifier with his Gibson, and the combination became the standard for blues playing and recording until the late 1980s.

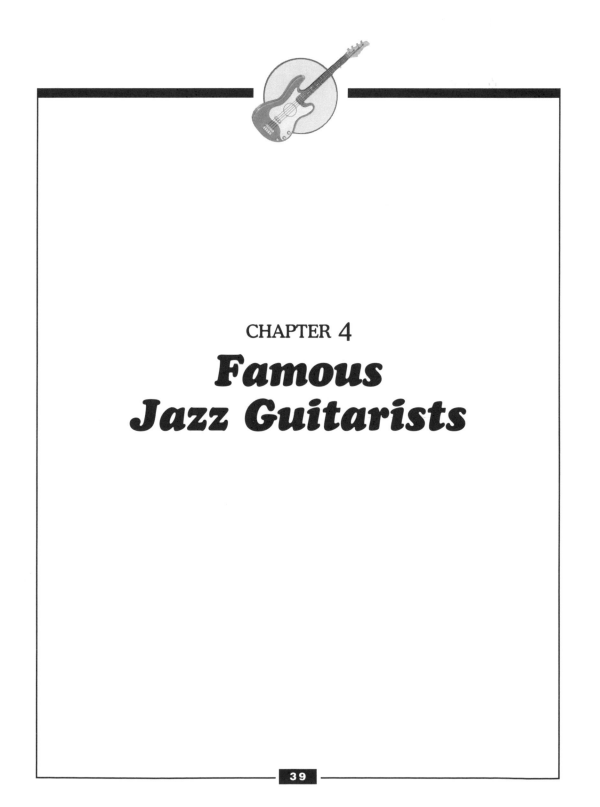

CHAPTER 4

Famous Jazz Guitarists

Django Reinhardt (1910–1953)

Django is considered the first major figure in jazz who was not American. That he was a guitarist, considered a lowly part of the rhythm section, is even more remarkable.

Born of a musical gypsy family in Belgium, he actually spent his childhood in a shantytown gypsy encampment outside of Paris. By the age of twelve he was playing banjo and violin on various gigs, and his first recordings, in 1928, were with an accordionist and someone playing slide whistle.

That same year he had an accident with a candle in his caravan, and was momentarily trapped in a blazing inferno. He was so badly burned he was bedridden for eighteen months, and his left hand was so injured it did not seem likely that he would ever play a musical instrument again.

What he did next was an indication of sheer genius and willpower. He came up with a completely radical way of playing the guitar using his two uninjured fingers on his left hand, barring the guitar neck occasionally with the fused stumps of the rest of his fingers, which gave his playing a harmonically distinctive "modern" sound. He also developed his right-hand technique, and his famous liquid chromatic runs were achieved by coordinating one shift of a left-hand finger with a down or up stroke of his plectrum in his right hand, for each note of the phrase.

His first recordings on guitar were made in 1931 as an accompanist to a singer. Accustomed to listening to and playing the improvised forms of gypsy music, he was fascinated with American jazz and its parallels to flamenco. It's more than likely he was listening to recordings of Duke Ellington, Louis Armstrong, and guitarist Lonnie Johnson, and violinist Joe Venuti and his sides with guitarist Eddie Lang, who also recorded some classic guitar duets with Lonnie Johnson.

By 1935 he had attracted the attention of visiting American musicians after he recorded with Coleman Hawkins and Michel Warlop's group. Record dates with Hawkins, Benny Carter, Dicky Wells, Eddie South, and Bill Coleman resulted in some classic recordings. In 1934, the Quintette Du Hot Club De France was formed, featuring Django on lead guitar, two rhythm guitars, a bass player, and violinist Stephane Grappelli.

That Django and Grappelli work well on disc is clearly evident. That they distrusted each other for the whole of their playing career is not. Django was fiery, emotionally powerful, and a naturally inventive improviser, but he was also impetuous and unpredictable. Grappelli was his opposite—cool, elegant, the "straw boss" of the group who made it all happen behind the scenes.

At the outbreak of World War II in 1939, the group was in London. Grappelli stayed in England, while Django returned to Paris. Ironically, despite the fact that the Nazi's despised jazz, after they occupied France in 1940, jazz seemed to flourish. Django reorganized the Hot Club of France, replacing one of the guitarists with a drummer, and Grappelli with a clarinet player.

Django had ambitions to compose for larger groups, but he was handicapped by the fact that he could neither read nor write music, and was dependent on others to take down his musical dictation.

Coming to America

After the war, Django went to America for a series of concerts. He expected to be feted as a conquering hero, but the audiences were cool to his antics. He brought no guitar with him, for example, and people had to rush around finding one for him to play. At his first concert, with Duke Ellington's band at Carnegie Hall, he was so late that Ellington was forced to offer an embarrassed apology for Django's nonappearance. Shortly after, Django strolled on stage and began to play.

Adopting Electric

In 1946 Django reunited with Grappelli, although he continued to play with other lineups as well. The major change in his career was his adoption of the electric guitar.

From 1937 onward, he had played a Selmer Maccaferri, a specially designed guitar that was louder than the normal acoustic instrument. After his American adventure, he fitted a "Charlie Christian" bar pickup on the Maccaferri, before eventually going all electric in 1950.

FACTS

The Selmer Maccaferri, made famous by Django Reinhardt, had a D-shaped sound hole, a flat cutaway, and two-octave fingerboard. The internal strutting was developed to enhance the volume and sustain. The guitars were launched in 1932, but by the end of the 1940s, Django was using a Stimer pickup, attached to his Maccaferri, using a small combination amp to get an electric sound.

By this time his improvisation was being influenced by the newly emerging bebop style of Charlie Christian and Charlie Parker, with their more sophisticated and complex harmonies and rhythms. In the last couple of years of his life Django went into semi-retirement in the village of Samois-sur-Seine, spending his time fishing, painting, and playing billiards. Yet he continued to play with the emerging French bebop players like pianist Martial Solal and Raymond Fol, and alto saxophonist Hubert Fol. He recorded his last record on a purely electric instrument with this next generation of musicians.

On May 16, 1953, he finished playing at the Club St. Germain in Paris and caught the train to Avon, the station nearest to Samois. He went to a local bar for a drink and passed out. He was rushed to a hospital in Fontainebleu but soon died. Three days later he was buried in Samois, at the age of forty-three.

Charlie Christian (1916–1942)

Charles Christian was born July 29, 1916, in Bonham, Texas, into a musical family. His mother played piano as an accompaniment to silent movies, while his father sang and played both trumpet and guitar. Christian's brothers, Clarence and Edward, also played professionally.

The family moved to Oklahoma City in 1918, and Christian's first instrument was the trumpet, a choice that no doubt helped formulate the horn-style, single-note guitar improvising that later made him famous.

Novelist and family friend Ralph Ellison said that at the age of twelve, Christian "would amuse and amaze us at school with his first guitar—one that he made from a cigar box . . . playing his own riffs. But they were based on sophisticated chords and progressions that Blind Lemon Jefferson never knew."

Throughout Christian's early teens, he played in the family band and performed in Oklahoma City clubs. It was there that he first heard and met the great tenor saxophonist Lester Young. The meeting was a seminal moment for Christian.

"Lester Young didn't bring Charlie Christian out of some dark nowhere," Ralph Ellison commented. "[Charlie] was already out in the light. He may only have been twelve or thirteen when he was making those cigarbox guitars in manual training class, but no other cigar boxes ever made such sounds. Then he heard Lester and that, I think, was all he needed."

By the early 1930s Christian doubled on bass and guitar in a band fronted by his brother Eddie, and was busy learning solos of Django Reinhardt and Lonnie Johnson. After briefly leading his own band, he played bass and/or guitar with a variety of well-known regional bands.

FACTS

One of the first recognizable jazz guitarists was Brock Mumford, who can be seen in a rare picture of Buddy Bolden's New Orleans Jazz Band at the turn of the twentieth century.

Christian had been experimenting with amplifying the guitar for several years in an effort to get a saxophone sound. Guitarist Mary Osborne recalled hearing what she thought was a tenor saxophone being played in a club in Bismark, North Dakota, in 1934 and discovering it was Christian with a microphone attached to his guitar. But the second seminal moment in Christian's life was in 1937, when he discovered the electric guitar.

The amplified electric guitar was still an experimental novelty, although electric guitarist and trombone player Eddie Durham was already playing it as a solo instrument in Jimmie Lunceford's band. The new invention made the jazz guitar solo a practical reality for the first time. With the exception of Lonnie Johnson and Eddie Lang, guitarists were part of the rhythm section, strumming chords. Now, guitarists could revel in the volume and sustain provided by an amplifier—in other words, sound like a saxophone or trumpet.

Christian and Goodman

Christian quickly realized the potential the electric guitar unleashed, and he soon developed a "saxophone style" of playing, reminiscent of his hero, Lester Young.

He got himself a Gibson ES-150 (listed in 1936 at $77.50, including a 15-foot cord), and by 1938 he was playing electric guitar in the Al Trent Sextet. By 1939, Charlie Christian's innovative guitar style was admired by many influential musicians in the jazz circuit, including pianists Teddy Wilson and Norma Teagarden. Pianist Mary Lou Williams recommended him to record producer and jazz promoter John Hammond. In August 1939, Hammond arranged for Charlie to have an audition with Benny Goodman, known at the time as "the King of Swing," and Hammond's brother-in-law. Goodman, who was white, was not only a great clarinet player, he was also a pioneer in touring with a mixed-race swing band.

FACTS

Charlie Christian played a Gibson ES-150, launched in 1936, and based on the L-50 acoustic archtop with the addition of a heavy, large bar magnet pickup, and a tone and volume control. He later switched to the newer ES-250.

Goodman needed some convincing. As Hammond recalled, when Christian arrived in Los Angeles, Goodman was presented with a country bumpkin so to speak. Goodman gave Christian a cursory audition, asking him to comp on "Tea for Two" without allowing him time to plug in his amp. He wasn't impressed.

Hammond said that he decided to convince Goodman by sneaking Christian onstage later that night during a concert at the Victor Hugo. Goodman angrily launched into "Rose Room," a number he figured Christian wouldn't know. "After the opening choruses Goodman pointed to Christian to take a solo," Hammond wrote, "and the number which ordinarily lasted three minutes stretched out to forty-five! Everyone got up from tables and clustered around the bandstand, and there could be no doubt that perhaps the most spectacularly original soloist ever to play with Goodman had been launched."

Goodman was won over. Christian's presence turbocharged the group, and Goodman made the most of the guitarist's new sound. His first studio recordings with the band were in New York City on October 2, 1939, in a session that included "Rose Room," "Flying Home," and Christian's memorable solo on "Stardust." By 1940 he had recorded "Gone With What Wind," and "Air Mail Special," which featured snappy lines reminiscent of Django, and he had been voted Top Guitarist by *Metronome* magazine readers. While Goodman sometimes took credit for melodies actually composed by his sidemen, he nevertheless gave Christian partial credit for several classics, including "Seven Come Eleven," "Air Mail Special," and "Solo Flight."

Jam Sessions

The sextet made Christian a star in the jazz world, and helped legitimize and popularize the electric guitar as a jazz instrument. Some of Christian's last recordings were made in two after-hours joints in Harlem, in the cutting-edge hothouse environment of Minton's and of Monroe's Uptown House. They are considered by many to be the first recordings that show the 1930s swing style evolving into the fiery, harmonically and far more rhythmically complex bebop style.

Minton's, on West 118th Street, established by a retired sax player named Henry Minton, was located in a former dining room in the Hotel Cecil. The manager was a fellow saxophonist and former bandleader, Teddy Hill, who hired a rhythm section that included Thelonious Monk and Kenny Clarke. Jam sessions would sometimes last all night.

Christian was so into the jam sessions he bought a second amp to leave at Minton's. The band often included Kenny Kersey on piano, Kenny Clarke on drums, trumpeter Joe Guy, and bassist Nick Fenton. Private recordings made by a jazz enthusiast at Minton's reveal Charlie Christian at his most inventive and experimental, as on the extended "Swing to Bop."

An Early Death

In the summer of 1941, Christian developed the first signs of tuberculosis. He was forced to leave the Goodman band's tour of the Midwest and entered the Seaview Sanatorium on Staten Island. Count Basie's doctor kept an eye on him, while Teddy Hill came once a week bearing fried chicken and other goodies, and well-meaning friends sneaked him whisky and dope. He began to improve but found life dull, so one night he slipped out with some friends for off-limits carousing, caught a chill, and died. The date was March 2, 1942. He was twenty-five years old.

Christian was buried in a small cemetery in Bonham. Although the exact location of his grave is not known, a marker and headstone were erected in his honor in 1994.

The amazing thing about Christian is that he recorded for a mere three years, but managed in that short time to influence many generations of musicians. He has been cited as an influence by blues and rock musicians as well as jazz guitarists. His style may lack some of the technical virtuosity of some modern guitarists, but Christian's lively, inventive single-note playing helped popularize the electric guitar as a solo instrument and ushered in the era of Charlie Parker and bebop.

Barney Kessel (1923–)

Born in Muskogee, Oklahoma, Kessel took on Christian's mantle in the mid-1940s through to the late 1980s. An innovative guitarist, he followed and developed Charlie Christian's swing style of playing, developing the harmonic possibilities of the instrument in a way that clearly showed a guitar player could do anything a piano player could do, and sometimes better.

Kessel got his first guitar at age twelve and was playing gigs with all-black bands two years later. At sixteen he met and jammed with Charlie Christian, whose music he knew from recordings and radio broadcasts with Benny Goodman. A year later he left for Los Angeles to make it as a musician.

He got a job in Chico Marx's band, and in the mid-1940s he was featured with Charlie Parker and Lester Young. He was also featured with

Lionel Hampton in the Jazz at the Philharmonic concerts. By 1947 he had worked with a number of big bands, including Benny Goodman's and Artie Shaw's. That same year he went into the studio with Charlie Parker, and the results were some classic bebop recordings that established Kessel as an accomplished and confident musician.

In 1952 he joined the Oscar Peterson Trio for a Jazz at the Philharmonic tour that visited fourteen countries. He continued to record with Peterson and a score of other major jazz names. In the late 1950s and the 1960s, he became a major figure in the Los Angeles recording industry. His 1955 Trio record *Cry Me a River,* featuring singer Julie London, is a classic of its type. He also recorded a series of records called *The Poll Winners* with bass player Ray Brown and drummer Shelley Mann. The records were so-called because he and his partners consistently won jazz polls in *Down Beat*, *Esquire*, *Playboy*, *Metronome*, and *Melody Maker* magazines.

He continued to play jazz and tour until 1992, when he suffered a stroke that left him unable to play anymore. He continued to teach, however, and has regained his ability to speak and move.

FACTS

In 1934, Gibson introduced the large-bodied archtop Super 400, designed to give more volume.

Tal Farlow (1921–1998)

While working in the seminal Red Norvo Trio with vibes player Norvo and the bass player Charlie Mingus—Tal Farlow commented there were only two tempos the group played—fast, and even faster.

Farlow is one of the two major influential bebop guitar players who led jazz into the 1950s after Charlie Christian, inspired by Charlie Parker. The other was his long-time friend Jimmy Raney, although Farlow is often considered the slightly more influential of the two. Farlow's large hands helped him develop sophisticated chord voicings full of space and slight dissonances, while his inventive up-tempo single-note improvisations and imaginative use of artificial harmonics quickly won him a place as a major figure in jazz.

FACTS

Both Barney Kessel and Tal Farlow used the Gibson ES-350, the first electric archtop with a cutaway, which was launched in 1946.

Born in North Carolina, Farlow began playing professionally at the relatively late age of twenty-two. He apprenticed as a sign painter at the insistence of his guitar-playing father, and intermittently throughout his playing career he returned to that trade. A reticent, self-effacing man with a laconic, Southern sense of humor, he once commented that playing a jazz solo was "pretty much the same thing as painting a sign."

Farlow was essentially a self-taught musician, inspired by hearing Charlie Christian on the radio with Benny Goodman. He moved to New York and quickly fell under the influence of major bebop musicians like Charlie Parker and Bud Powell, whom he listened to and occasionally played music with in and around 52nd Street. He first came to prominence as a sideman with clarinetist Buddy DeFranco, but his breakthrough happened in 1949 when he joined the Red Norvo Trio (1949–1953) at the recommendation of guitarist Mundell Lowe. The trio was one of the first expressions of modern chamber jazz.

After Norvo, Farlow joined Artie Shaw's Gramercy Five and then led his own groups. He recorded several classic jazz records before marrying in 1958 and retiring from the limelight. He moved to Sea Bright, New Jersey, where he continued to play locally, teach, and work as a sign painter.

In the 1970s, he came out of retirement, contracted with Concord Records, and began to tour internationally again. In his declining years, he performed and recorded under the banner of the Great Guitars, with Herb Ellis, Charlie Byrd, and Barney Kessel. A fifty-eight-minute documentary, *Talmage Farlow*, was released by Lorenzo DeStefano. A compilation selected from Farlow's seven discs for Verve in the early 1950s, *Jazz Masters 41*, and *Tal*, also on Verve, are exemplary recordings of his work. He died of cancer in 1998.

Johnny Smith (1922–)

Smith, like Tal Farlow, another guitarist with long fingers, developed a distinctive style of guitar playing that was well captured on his 1952 hit record "Moonlight in Vermont," which also featured saxophonist Stan Getz. He worked with Benny Goodman in the early 1950s and established himself as a session musician at NBC in New York.

A self-taught musician who originally played trumpet, violin, and viola before switching to guitar, he incorporated classical phrasing and precise articulation. In the 1960s he moved to Colorado and opened a music store, taught, and maintained a lower profile, occasionally recording in New York.

FACTS

The Gibson ES-175 was launched in 1949. It remains a mainstay of fusion and jazz players to this day, and has been used by Jim Hall, Joe Pas, and Pat Metheny, to mention but three of thousands who used the guitar.

Jimmy Raney (1927–1995)

A definitive cool jazz guitarist and a fluid bop soloist with a quiet sound who had a great deal of inner fire, Raney was influenced by Charlie Christian, but his style grew to encompass not just Charlie Parker but also the Lennie Tristano school of "cool bop." Indeed, Raney was sometimes called the Lee Konitz of the guitar, after the famous alto player associated with Lennie Tristano.

As a soloist he emphasized lines inspired by those of Lester Young. He compensated for the emotional coolness of his improvisations by employing long melodic lines, cleanly articulated. One of the true innovators on his instrument, Raney exercised a profound influence upon guitarists of the 1950s.

Born in Louisville, Kentucky, he was influenced by his mother, who played guitar, and he studied with the guitarist Hayden Causey, whom he replaced in a band led by Jerry Wald. In 1944 he moved to Chicago, where he worked with pianist Lou Levy. In 1948 he joined Woody Herman's orchestra and recorded with Stan Getz.

After leaving Herman he played with Al Haig, Buddy DeFranco, Artie Shaw (1949–1950), and Terry Gibbs, then joined Getz's quintet. It was this group that brought him to prominence as he became known for his playing on several of Getz's important albums between 1951 and 1953. He replaced Tal Farlow in Red Norvo's Trio (1953–1954) and worked at the Blue Angel, New York, (1955–1960) in a trio led by the pianist Jimmy Lyon. He rejoined Getz in 1962, but remained with him only until the following year.

In the mid-1960s he was active in New York as a studio musician in radio and television before returning to Louisville in 1968. He later played at clubs in New York (1972), gave a recital at Carnegie Hall with Al Haig (1974), and toured internationally with Haig and his son Doug Raney, with whom he also recorded guitar duos. In the 1980s he performed and recorded as the leader of his own groups, which included his son, although encroaching deafness hampered his ability to play in his last few years. He died in 1995.

Jim Hall (1930–)

A cool-toned, subtle guitarist whose playing seems to be the jazz equivalent of a Japanese painting, Jim Hall has been an inspiration to guitarists—some of whom, like Bill Frisell, sound nothing like him.

Inspired (as almost all the guitarists of his generation were) by Charlie Christian, and by the tenor saxophonist Lester Young, Jim Hall attended the Cleveland Institute of Music and studied classical guitar in Los Angeles with Vincente Gomez. He was a founding member of the Chico Hamilton Quintet (1955), and in 1956 joined the Jimmy Giuffre Three.

After touring with Ella Fitzgerald in 1960 and sometimes forming duos with Lee Konitz, he joined Sonny Rollins's quartet in 1961, and recorded the classic guitar-tenor saxophone quartet *The Bridge*. He next co-led a quartet with Art Farmer (1962), and recorded on an occasional basis with Paul Desmond. He then became a New York studio musician.

He has mostly been a leader since then, and has also worked on his own projects for a variety of record labels, including two classic duet albums with pianist Bill Evans. A self-titled collaboration with Pat Metheny was released in 1999.

John L. "Wes" Montgomery (1925–1968)

Considered one of the great jazz guitarists, Wes Montgomery admitted to influences that included Charlie Christian, and then later the saxophonist John Coltrane, with whom he played briefly in an unrecorded group.

Wes's development and use of octaves became both influential and a trademark, but it took Wes a long time to become an "overnight success," achieving commercial success with his Verve recordings during his last few years, only to die of a heart attack prematurely.

Like his idol, Charlie Christian, Wes came from a musical family and taught himself guitar by learning the solos of Charlie Christian and Django Reinhardt, from whom he developed the idea of playing octaves. He tried to use a pick in the conventional style but eventually opted to use his thumb because he preferred the thick warm sound it produced. He toured with Lionel Hampton's big band during 1948 through 1950, and can be heard on a few broadcasts from the period. Then he returned to Indianapolis, where he played in relative obscurity during much of the 1950s, working a day job and playing at clubs most nights.

He recorded with his brothers, pianist and vibraphonist Buddy and bass player Monk, during 1957 through 1959, and he made his first album, *The Wes Montgomery Trio* (1959), with organist Mel Rhyne.

In 1960, the release of his album *The Incredible Jazz Guitar of Wes Montgomery* made him famous in the jazz world. Later that year he spent some time playing with the John Coltrane Sextet.

Montgomery's Riverside dates (1959–1963) are among his most inventive jazz recordings, in small-group sessions with such sidemen as George Shearing, Tommy Flanagan, James Clay, Victor Feldman, Hank Jones, Johnny Griffin, and Mel Rhyne.

From 1964 through 1966 he moved to Verve and recorded a series of orchestral dates with arranger Don Sebesky and producer Creed Taylor.

These records popularized him with the general listening audience, widening his appeal from a pure jazz base. In 1967 he continued this trend, signing with Creed Taylor at A&M, where he recorded three best-selling albums that featured him playing pop melodies backed by strings and woodwinds.

He died of a heart attack at the height of his success. However, Wes Montgomery's influence is still felt through many young guitarists, notably Pat Metheny.

Pat Martino (1944-)

One of the most original of the jazz-based guitarists to emerge in the 1960s, Martino began playing professionally when he was fifteen. He worked early on with groups led by Willis Jackson, Red Holloway, and a series of organists, including Don Patterson, Jimmy Smith, Jack McDuff, Richard "Groove" Holmes, and Jimmy McGriff. After playing with John Handy (1966), he absorbed the influences of avant-garde jazz, rock, pop, and world music into his advanced hard bop style. His debut album *El Hombre* (1967) exploded onto the scene.

Martino made a remarkable comeback after brain surgery in 1980 to correct an aneurysm that caused him to completely forget how to play. It took years but he regained his ability, partly by listening to his records. He did not resume playing until 1984, making his recording comeback with 1987's *The Return*.

Joe Pass (1929–1994)

A hard-hitting bebop guitarist early on in his career, Pass became known as a great solo performer. His outstanding technique, recorded in the *Virtuoso* series of records on the Pablo label, gave him the deserved popular fame and renown that had eluded him in his earlier career.

Hailing from Philadelphia (and influenced by the troubled but virtuoso jazz guitarist Billy Bean), Pass began playing in a few swing bands and was with Charlie Barnet for a time in 1947. After serving in the military, Pass became a drug addict, spending nearly a decade in and out of prison.

While recovering at the Synanon Halfway House, along with other musicians, the Santa Monica city council decided to disband the house. In order to make money to establish the halfway house outside the city limits, the talents of the recovering addicts were put to use. They borrowed instruments and went into a recording studio to record a series of original jazz tunes. *Sounds of Synanon* (1962) made such a stir that it brought Pass instant recognition as a new jazz talent. He followed this record with his first as a leader, *Catch Me* and then the seminal *For Django*, before going on to record several other albums for Pacific Jazz and World Pacific.

In 1974 he signed with Norman Granz's Pablo label and issued *Virtuoso,* the first of his solo guitar recordings. The record got great attention. After that he recorded both unaccompanied and with small groups, including artists Neils Hennig, Osted Pedersen, Sarah Vaughan, Ella Fitzgerald, Duke Ellington, Oscar Peterson, Milt Jackson, and Dizzy Gillespie, until his death from cancer.

FACTS

Guitarist John McLaughlin popularized both the fiberglass, round-backed Ovation, as well as the Gibson EDS-1275, a double-necked guitar comprised of a six string and a twelve string.

George Benson (1943–)

Born in Pittsburgh, Pennsylvania, Benson began performing as a young teenager, singing in nightclubs and recording several cuts for RCA. In 1960 Benson formed a rock band, but he soon became more interested in jazz, awed by performers like Charlie Parker and Charlie Christian. After a stint in Brother Jack McDuff's Band, Benson formed his own jazz group in 1965, recording several albums for Columbia and appearing on Miles Davis's *Miles in the Sky*. In 1967, Benson moved to Verve and then to producer Creed Taylor's own CTI label for much of the 1970s. Benson's guitar playing won over jazz fans and critics, earning comparisons to Wes Montgomery and Charlie Christian, among others.

In the late 1970s, Benson recorded with Warner Bros., focusing on his soulful Nat King Cole–inspired singing. Beginning with the Top 10 1976 album *Breezin'* and its hit single "This Masquerade," Benson began producing a series of pop albums, working with producer Quincy Jones on what was to be Benson's biggest album yet, *Give Me the Night* (1980).

Following a career path similar to Wes Montgomery's, Benson lost touch with hard-core jazz fans, but found himself becoming more popular and commercially successful with a broader audience. By the 1980s, Benson's vocal talent was more well known than his amazing guitar playing. However, by the early 1990s, he began to re-emphasize his jazz guitar ability.

Jack Wilkins (1944–)

Wilkins has been a part of the New York jazz scene for more than four decades. His flawless technique and imaginative chordal approach have inspired collaborations with Chet Baker, Sarah Vaughan, Bob Brookmeyer, Buddy Rich, and many others.

A native of Brooklyn, Wilkins began playing guitar at the age of thirteen. His influences included Johnny Smith, Django Reinhardt, Charlie Christian, Wes Montgomery, Joe Pass, Bill Evans, Clifford Brown, and Freddie Hubbard.

His first album as a leader (*Windows*, Mainstream, 1973; available in transcription from Hal Leonard Corporation) was critically acclaimed as a dazzling, seminal guitar trio. Later recordings—*Merge, Mexico, Call Him Reckless, Alien Army, Keep in Touch,* and *Trioart*—feature the Brecker Brothers, Eddie Gomez, Jack De Johnette, Al Foster, Phil Woods, Kenny Drew Jr., and many others.

In recent years, Wilkins has played at international festivals and in partnership with many jazz greats, including Stanley Turrentine, Jimmy Heath, The Mingus Epitaph, 5 Guitars Play Mingus (in which he was the primary arranger), and bassist Eddie Gomez. A consummate accompanist, Wilkins has played and recorded with renowned singers such as Mel

Torme, Ray Charles, Morgana King, Sarah Vaughan, Tony Bennett, Manhattan Transfer, Nancy Marano, and Jay Clayton.

Wilkins was awarded an NEA grant in recognition of his work and contribution to the guitar. He has been widely and prominently profiled and featured in such publications as *Guitar Player*, *Just Jazz Guitar*, *Downbeat*, *20th Century Guitar*, and *Leonard Feather's Jazz Encyclopedia*. Recently, Wilkins was invited to the Smithsonian Institution to be part of the "Blue Guitars" exhibit, and was featured on the PSI, the first live jazz Internet concert. He was also featured as part of the JVC festival tributes to Johnny Smith, Tal Farlow, and Herb Ellis.

Wilkins lives in Manhattan and teaches at the New School and the Manhattan School of Music. He is also a judge for the prestigious Monk Institute Guitar Competitions in Washington, and conducts seminars and guitar clinics in New York and abroad.

FACTS

Alan Holdsworth, the remarkable British jazz-rock fusion player, plays a SynthAxe on his album *Atavachron* (1986). The SynthAxe is an innovative synthesizer guitar with a fretboard touch system. Other guitarists who have extensively used guitar synthesizers include John Abercrombie and Pat Metheny.

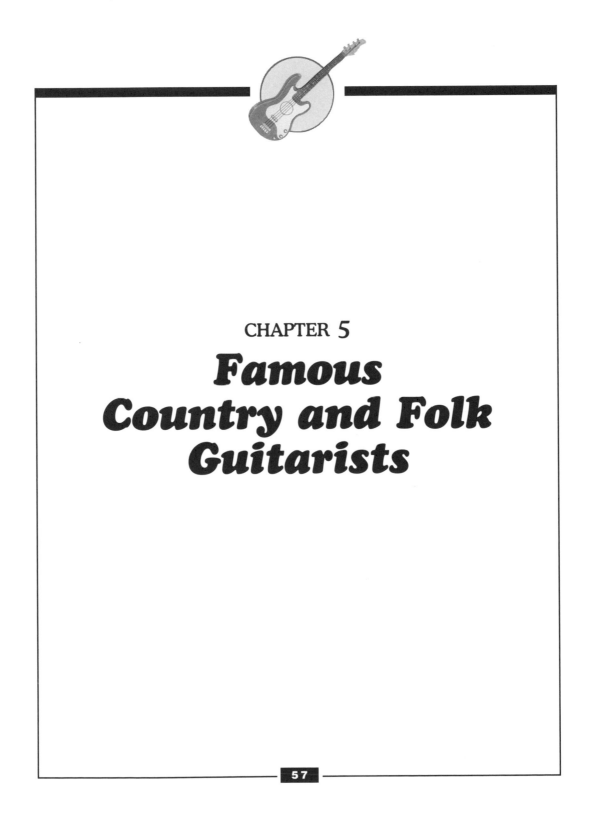

CHAPTER 5

Famous Country and Folk Guitarists

Arthel "Doc" Watson (1923–)

Arguably, there have been three influential country folk guitar players in the twentieth century: Merle Travis, Chet Atkins, and Doc Watson, a brilliant flat-picking guitarist from Deep Gap, North Carolina.

Unlike Travis and Atkins, Watson was middle-aged before he gained any attention through the release of his first album, *The Doc Watson Family,* in 1963. The record is a mixture of folk, country, and bluegrass and was influential on guitar players in the early 1960s. His appearances at the Newport Folk Festivals in 1963 and 1964 stunned musicians, who were amazed to hear such virtuoso playing from someone from the backwoods. Performers of folk music and country alike—such as Ricky Skaggs, Vince Gill, Clarence White, Emmylou Harris, and many others—acknowledge Watson's influence on them. Watson has provided a further service to country and folk music by sharing an almost encyclopedic knowledge of many American traditional songs. While Merle Travis and Chet Atkins started on acoustic guitars and moved to electric, before Watson's "discovery" during the folk revival in the early 1960s, he played electric in a local all-purpose band that performed current rock, swing, country—and, of course, folk music.

Watson was struck blind at an early age. When he was ten, his father gave him a homemade fretless banjo, which Doc played consistently for the next three years. Around the same time, he began attending the School for the Blind in Raleigh, North Carolina. At the age of thirteen Doc began playing guitar, and six months later Doc and his older brother Linney began performing on street corners, singing traditional numbers.

By his late teens, Watson learned finger-picking from his neighbor, Olin Miller. In 1941, Watson joined a band that had a regular radio program in Lenoir, North Carolina. At this show he earned his nickname; one of the announcers referred to the guitarist as "Doc" during the broadcast. For the next six years he played around North Carolina.

In 1947, he married Rosa Lee Carlton, the daughter of fiddler Gaither W. Carlton. To pay the bills, he worked as a piano tuner. In 1953, Watson joined the supporting band of a local pianist and railroad worker named Jack Williams, where he played electric guitar and performed a variety of music, from country to rock and pop. After staying with Jack for eight years, Watson joined the Clarence Ashley String Band.

From 1964 onward, Watson recorded nearly one record a year through 1970. No sooner had interest in folk music waned than Watson was back in great demand because of the three-disc *Will the Circle Be Unbroken*, a watershed album in 1972 created by the Nitty Gritty Dirt Band, which featured Watson, Travis, Roy Acuff, and a Who's Who of country greats. Merle Watson, Doc's son and a serious talent in his own right, began appearing with his father regularly. The result was good enough for them to win two Grammys for traditional music, in 1973 and 1974.

Father and son played together for more than fifteen years, until Merle died tragically on the family farm in 1985. Following his son's death, Doc Watson continued with his appearances, showcasing his beautiful voice, his great instrumental talent, and his mastery of traditional material.

FACTS

Maybelle Carter, of the seminal folk group the Carter Family—comprised of Maybelle, her sister Sara, and Sara's husband, A. P. Carter—played a Gibson L-5 archtop, first produced in 1922. The instrument was revolutionary, modeled after mandolins and violins, with F-shaped holes rather than one round sound hole. Maybelle's playing was sometimes described as "church licks" and the technique was dubbed the "Carter Scratch."

Chet Atkins (1924–2001)

An asthma sufferer throughout his youth, Atkins was a sickly child from a humble background in Tennessee. When his parents separated when he was ten, Atkins moved to Georgia to live with his father, hoping the climate would be easier on his asthma.

His father was a music teacher and songleader with a number of traveling evangelists, and his brother Jimmy—thirteen years Chet's senior—was himself an accomplished guitar player. Atkins's first instrument was a ukulele strung with wire from a screen door; he then graduated to an inexpensive Sears Silvertone. Atkins said that his childhood adversity was a significant motivator in driving him to be "the greatest at what he did."

A series of performances on local radio stations, as well as the popular Old Dominion Barn Dance, ended poorly, because his sophisticated musicianship was at odds with the simple twangy "hillbilly" guitar the producers wanted. His break came in 1947 with a gig with the legendary Carter Family at the Grand Ole Opry, where his talents were finally appreciated. After that his close association with RCA in Nashville led to Atkins becoming a sought-after session player, working on records by some of the great pioneers of both country and rock-and-roll, including the Everly Brothers and Elvis Presley.

Atkins joined RCA as a vice president and staff producer and almost single-handedly created the smooth sound that became known as the "Nashville Sound," scoring major hits with nearly every country star of the era. Upon leaving RCA, Chet continued his highly successful career as a recording artist, signing with Columbia Records.

Hank Williams (1923–1953)

Williams is considered the father of contemporary country music. He was a major star by the age of twenty-five and dead at the age of twenty-nine. He began recording in Nashville in 1946 with a lineup that featured electric and acoustic guitars, and he helped set the scene for the rock-and-roll revolution of the 1950s.

In four short years, he established the rules for all the country performers that followed him—and, in the process, much of popular music. Williams wrote a body of songs that hit the Top 10 charts and became popular classics, and his direct, emotional lyrics and vocals became the standard for most popular performers.

FACTS

Jimmie Rodgers (the "singing brakeman") is considered one of country music's first big stars. However, he described himself as someone "who couldn't read a note, keep time, or play the right chords."

Merle Travis (1917–1983)

Virtually without peer as a guitarist and songwriter, Travis was such a unique stylist, he had an instrumental style ("Travis picking") named after him. Only Chet Atkins even comes close to the influence that Travis had on guitarists and country music.

Born in Rosewood, Kentucky, to a family of impoverished coal miners, he turned this experience, coupled with a phrase that Travis's father used to describe their lives, into the song "Sixteen Tons." As a songwriter, his originals, including "Sixteen Tons," crossed over as popular standards in the hands of other artists. He was also influential in the development of rock-and-roll, and recorded a number of Top 10 hits and novelty songs.

His first instrument was a five-string banjo, and he was lucky enough to live next door to Ike Everly, later the father of Don and Phil (the Everly Brothers), and Mose Rager, who played in a unique three-finger guitar style that had developed in that part of Kentucky.

Travis's repertory soon included blues, ragtime, and popular tunes, although he paid the bills by working in the Civilian Conservation Corps as a teenager. His break came during a visit to his brother's home in Evansville, Indiana, in 1935, where his chance to entertain at a local dance resulted in membership in a couple of local bands and a chance to appear on a local radio station.

In 1937, he landed a permanent broadcasting gig at Cincinnati's WLW until World War II forced it to disband. As a member of the Drifting Pioneers, Travis acquired a national following, and also began playing with Grandpa Jones and the Delmore Brothers in a gospel quartet called the Brown's Ferry Four. While touring with Jones, Travis visited a church in Cincinnati and heard the sermon that became the song "That's All."

He spent a short stint in the Marines, but was quickly discharged and returned to Cincinnati. By early 1945 he was in Los Angeles, where he began making appearances in Charles Starrett's Western movies and playing with Ray Whitley's Western Swing band. In 1946 he released the topical song "No Vacancy"—dealing with the displacement of returning veterans—along with "Cincinnati Lou," and earned a double-sided hit. His next major project was a concept album, *Folk Songs of the Hills*, which was intended to compete with Burl Ives's successful folk recordings.

Released as a set of four 78 rpm discs, the record was released in 1947, but considered a failure. However, it yielded several classics, among them the Travis originals "Sixteen Tons," "Dark as a Dungeon," and "Over by Number Nine." It also introduced such standards as "Nine Pound Hammer," and it became a unique document, depicting a beautiful all-acoustic solo guitar performance by this virtuoso. Using his thumb to stop the bottom two strings allowed him to create mobile upper chords, teamed with jazzy voicings, open strings, and rolling fast arpeggios. This style inspired generations of guitarists.

FACTS

When she was a child, Elizabeth Cotton wrote "Freight Train," one of the most famous American folksongs. However, she didn't release her first album until she was sixty-three, in 1958.

Pete Seeger (1919–)

Along with Woody Guthrie, singer/songwriter Pete Seeger is considered one of the pioneers of modern folk music. Seeger is synonymous with the folk boom of the late 1950s and early 1960s, and he helped transform folk from an orally transmitted body of traditional songs found mainly among rural dwellers to a mass-market form of entertainment, popular on college campuses and in New York coffeehouses.

Born in New York City, the son of Julliard musicologist Charles Seeger, one of the first researchers to investigate non-Western music, Pete Seeger was educated at a series of exclusive private schools, including Harvard, where he majored in sociology. He began playing banjo in his teens, and developed an intense interest in folk music that only grew over time. In 1938, he shocked his parents by dropping out of college to hitchhike across the United States, meeting many legendary folk musicians along the way, including Leadbelly and Woody Guthrie.

When he returned to New York in 1940, Seeger formed the Almanac Singers, a rotating cast of folk singers (at times including Woody Guthrie) that merged politically progressive lyrics with folk tunes. They performed mainly at union rallies, strikes, and similar events. The Almanac Singers disbanded during World War II, when Seeger was drafted.

After serving in the military for several years, Seeger returned to New York in 1948 and formed the Weavers, the first mainstream American folk group. The Weavers scored several big hits in the late 1940s and early 1950s, including 1948's "Goodnight Irene," which stayed at Number 1 for weeks, setting a chart record not broken until the 1970s.

During the McCarthy-era Red Scare, the Weavers suffered boycotts because of their left-leaning views. This severely curtailed their success. However, in 1955, the group gave a legendary performance at Carnegie Hall, which set the stage for the urban folk boom of the late 1950s.

From 1958 onward, Seeger opted for a solo career, and he quickly became a star in his own right. Known for songs such as "If I Had a Hammer" (a hit for Peter, Paul, and Mary), "Where Have All the Flowers Gone," "Turn! Turn! Turn!" (later popularized by the Byrds), "Guantanamera," and, most famous, "We Shall Overcome," Seeger became a fixture at civil rights rallies, college campuses, labor strikes, and anti-war protests, where audiences would often sing along so loud that Seeger himself could hardly be heard.

In 1961, Seeger signed with Columbia Records, and his popularity grew even further over the next few years. Toward the end of the 1960s, Seeger shifted away from typical American folk, embracing African music, Latin-American folksongs, and other forms of world music. He wrote several famous "how to" books on acoustic guitar and banjo, and became active in the nascent environmental movement, drawing attention to pollution of the Hudson River through boating trips. He later formed the activist group Clearwater, which teaches schoolchildren about water pollution.

FACTS

Twelve-string folk guitarist Leo Kottke was inspired by classical composers such as Stravinsky. He played a Gibson B-45 twelve-string on his first album before changing to a Martin D-28 twelve-string, and then custom-built guitars with cutaways. Kottke's intense energy and crossover style incorporated open tunings and low bass notes.

Woody Guthrie (1912–1967)

Born in Okemah, Oklahoma, Guthrie described the small frontier town in Okfuskee County like this: "Okemah was one of the singiest, square dancingest, drinkingest, yellingest, preachingest, walkingest, talkingest, laughingest, cryingest, shootingest, fist fightingest, bleedingest, gamblingest, gun, club and razor carryingest of our ranch towns and farm towns, because it blossomed out into one of our first Oil Boom Towns."

His father, Charles, was a cowboy, land speculator, and local politician. The family's financial and physical ruin and his mother's institutionalization because of Huntingdon's Chorea devastated Guthrie, creating a uniquely wry and rambling outlook on life.

A skinny, wiry man, with a head of unruly curly hair, Guthrie was a keen observer of the world around him. In 1931, when Okemah's boomtown period went bust, Guthrie left for Texas. In 1933, in the panhandle town of Pampa, he married Mary Jennings, and together they had three children. The Great Depression and the Great Dust Storm of 1935 made it impossible to make a living. Driven by a search for a better life, Guthrie joined the westward migration of dust bowl refugees known as "Okies."

Without money and hungry, he hitchhiked, rode freight trains, and even walked to California, developing a love for traveling on the "open road"—a practice he would repeat often. By the time he arrived in California, in 1937, he had experienced the intense hatred of Californians for the Okies and for other "outsiders" who were flooding the state.

Guthrie's identification with outsiders soon found its way into his songwriting, as evident in his Dust Bowl Ballads such as "I Ain't Got No Home," "Talking Dust Bowl Blues," and "Tom Joad and Hard Travelin'."

His 1937 radio broadcasts on KFVD, Los Angeles, and XELO (just over the border in Mexico) brought Guthrie wide public attention. It also gave him a platform from which he could develop his talent for controversial social commentary and criticism on topics ranging from corrupt politicians, lawyers, and businessmen to praising the humanist principles of Jesus Christ, Pretty Boy Floyd, and union organizers.

Never one to stay in one place for too long, Guthrie headed east for New York City in 1939, where he was quickly embraced by leftist organizations, artists, writers, musicians, and other intellectuals.

Meeting and mingling with artists such as Leadbelly, Cisco Houston, Burl Ives, Pete Seeger, Will Geer, Sonny Terry, Brownie McGhee, Josh White, Millard Lampell, Bess Hawes, Sis Cunningham, and others, Guthrie took such social causes as union organizing, anti-fascism, and strengthening the communist party. Generally, he fought for the things he and his friends believed in the only way he knew how: through political songs of protest.

In 1940, folklorist Alan Lomax recorded Guthrie for the Library of Congress in a series of conversations and songs. The Almanac Singers, the politically radical singing group of the late 1940s, would later reform as the Weavers, the most commercially successful and influential folk music group of the late 1940s and early 1950s.

Finally, disillusioned with New York's radio and entertainment industry, Guthrie headed down south.

With the final dissolution of his first marriage, and despite Guthrie's constant traveling and performing, he nevertheless courted an already married young Martha Graham dancer named Marjorie Mazia. This relationship provided Guthrie with a level of domestic stability and encouragement he had not previously known, enabling him to complete and publish his first novel, *Bound for Glory* (1943). A semiautobiographical account of his Dust Bowl years, *Bound for Glory* received critical acclaim. Together, Guthrie and Marjorie had four children: Cathy, who died at age four; Arlo (who grew up to be a famous folk singer in his own right, with a major hit in the 1960s, "Alice's Restaurant"); Joady; and Nora.

An ardent anti-fascist, during World War II Guthrie served in both the Merchant Marine and the Army, shipping out to sea on several occasions with his buddies Cisco Houston and Jimmy Longhi.

In 1946, Guthrie settled in Coney Island, New York, with his wife and children. Soon his behavior and health began to deteriorate, becoming increasingly erratic and creating tensions in his personal and professional life. He moved to California, remarried for a third time, and then returned to New York. He was eventually diagnosed with

Huntington's Chorea, the same degenerative disease that had taken his mother from him. For the next thirteen years he was in and out of hospitals. Finally, on October 3, 1967, at Creedmoor State Hospital in Queens, New York, Woody Guthrie died.

Popular and folk musicians such as Bruce Springsteen, Billy Bragg, Wilco, Ani DiFranco, and countless others continue to draw inspiration from Woody Guthrie, reinterpreting and reinvigorating his songs for new audiences. The Smithsonian Institution and the Woody Guthrie Foundation and Archives have collaborated on a major traveling exhibition about Guthrie's life and legacy, allowing thousands of people to view for themselves Guthrie's artwork, writings, and songs.

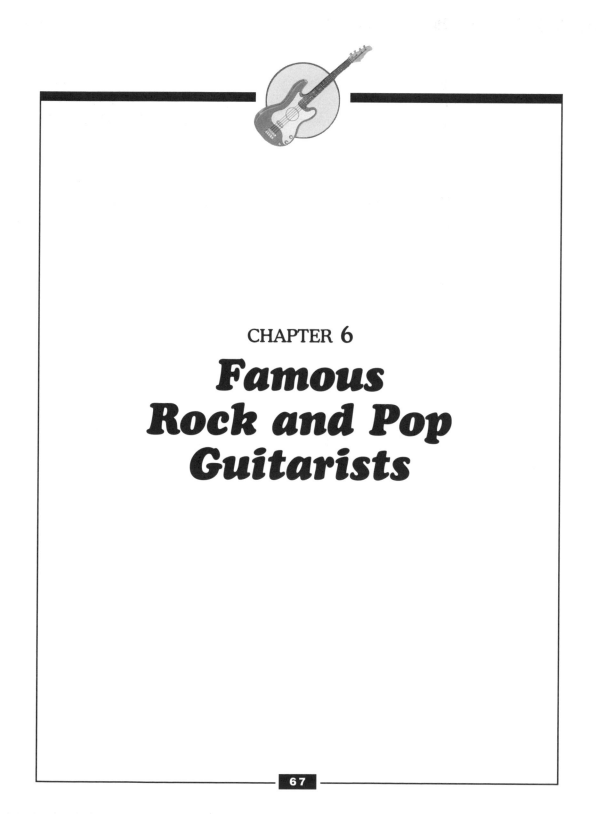

CHAPTER 6

Famous Rock and Pop Guitarists

Chuck Berry (1926-)

Hailed as the "Father of Rock and Roll," Chuck Berry's distinctive guitar playing, songwriting, and showmanship have influenced every rock-and-roll musician to follow him.

He grew up singing in a Baptist church in St. Louis, Missouri, and he absorbed influences as diverse as Robert Johnson, Charlie Christian, and Muddy Waters. Adapting the concept of boogie-woogie piano to the guitar, his first big hit was "Maybellene" in 1955. He then recorded a series of hits that defined rock. He was the first person to be inducted into the Rock and Roll Hall of Fame in 1986, and is a member of the Songwriters Hall of Fame.

His song "Johnny B. Goode" is on the copper records aboard the *Voyager* space probes, launched into outer space in 1977 to reach out to the universe with the best of our culture. In 1985, Chuck Berry entered the Blues Foundation's Hall of Fame.

Eric Clapton (1945-)

Clapton is possibly the most prominent rock guitarist to have emerged from England since the 1960s. At an early stage, his style showed the influences of bluesmen like Big Bill Broonzy, Robert Johnson, and Muddy Waters. His song "After Midnight" is one of 500 songs that shaped rock-and-roll according to the Rock and Roll Hall of Fame

In 1963, Clapton joined the seminal R&B group The Yardbirds. Two years later he left the band because he felt that they had become too much of a pop group, making room for Jeff Beck and Jimmy Page, two more guitarists who would become superstars of the British rock and blues scene.

Clapton went to California and joined John Mayall's Bluesbreakers. (Mick Fleetwood, John McVie, and Peter Green, the nucleus of Fleetwood Mac, also played with Mayall.) A year later, Clapton returned to London to form Cream, with bass player Jack Bruce and drummer Ginger Baker.

Following the breakup of Cream in 1968, Clapton formed Blind Faith with his neighbor, Steve Winwood, and ex-Cream drummer Ginger Baker.

Blind Faith didn't last long either, and Clapton's next public appearance was as a member of John Lennon's Plastic Ono Band at the Rock n' Roll Revival Show in Toronto.

In 1970, Clapton formed his own band, Derek and the Dominos, and fell in love with Pattie Harrison, the wife of his close friend George Harrison. In fact, it was Pattie who inspired Eric to write the classic song "Layla." (Clapton eventually married and divorced Pattie.) Clapton retired from the music business for a while, while he dealt with a drug problem.

In 1990, Clapton won a *Billboard* Music Award for Top Album Rock Artist, but also lost several members of his road crew and his friend Stevie Ray Vaughan in a helicopter crash. In February, 1991, Clapton won his first solo Grammy Award for Best Rock Vocal Male for "Bad Love." The following month, his four-year-old son was killed after falling out a high-rise window. In 1993, Clapton took home six Grammy Awards for his *Unplugged* album.

Jimi Hendrix (1942–1970)

One of the greatest—if not *the* greatest—rock guitarists of all time, Hendrix outshone his contemporaries, reinventing the sound and concept of playing the electric guitar. Born in Seattle, he was drawn to blues and rock through radio and records. He got his first guitar at the age of twelve and was playing with local bands by the time he was sixteen. After serving in Vietnam during the early 1960s, he returned to America and turned professional in 1962.

He was a sideman for a number of R&B artists, such as Little Richard, Ike and Tina Turner, and the Isley Brothers, but Hendrix felt his talents weren't being used to their best abilities, so he broke out on his own. Hendrix moved to New York in 1965, playing in various bars and clubs, while hooking up with blues rocker John Hammond, Jr. He formed his first band, Jimmy James and the Blue Flames. While playing in Club Wha? in Greenwich Village one night, he was approached by the Animals's bass player, Chas Chandler, who convinced Hendrix to move to London.

Hendrix Overseas

Hendrix arrived in London in September of 1966, and Chandler became his manager and worked with him on his first solo gig. An extraordinary guitarist and spectacular showman, Hendrix was an immediate sensation. Bringing drummer Mitch Mitchell and bassist Noel Redding on board, the Jimi Hendrix Experience was born. Its first live dates were played in France, and then they went into the studio.

The Experience incorporated R&B and soul and molded those sounds into what became the epitome of psychedelia, just becoming the signature fashion of the late 1960s.

Hendrix's debut single was "Hey Joe." During the session Hendrix met Roger Mayer, an electronics engineer who had developed new sound effects for the guitar. These effects can be heard on their next single, "Purple Haze."

FACTS

Jimi Hendrix played left-handed, though he played a standard right-hand model Fender Stratocaster—as well as a Gibson Flying V and a Les Paul—upside down, though strung the traditional way, and tuned down a semitone, like Stevie Ray Vaughan. Hendrix's main amplifiers were Marshall 100-watt models with two four-by-twelve cabinets, and he often used fuzz pedal, wah-wah, an Octavia, and a Uni-vibe built or modified by engineer Roger Mayer.

Hendrix exploded onto the scene with his debut album, *Are You Experienced?* (1967), which he followed up with *Axis: Bold As Love* later that same year. Both took Hendrix's guitar playing and songwriting to new levels. Each song put Hendrix into the U.K. Top 10, and they earned him a top spot at the Monterey Pop Festival in the United States later that year. Drawing on the R&B showmanship of his early years, Hendrix commanded everyone's attention while he played his guitar behind his back, with his teeth, and over his head. One of his set's highlights was "Wild Thing," when he smashed his guitar against amplifiers to generate atonal chords, before pouring lighter fluid over the instrument, setting it on fire, and smashing it to pieces, stunning his audience.

Experimentation

Everyone from music moguls to teenagers were taken by Hendrix's experimentation. He used distorted riffs, mind-blowing feedback, and thumping wah-wah pedals to make his music speak to the crowd.

In 1969 he played Woodstock with an extended lineup that included Billy Cox replacing Noel Redding on bass. The performance was electrifying and captured on film. It climaxed with an anti–Vietnam War version of "The Star Spangled Banner," filled with screeching avant-garde notes and feedback, becoming a grotesque parody of the original.

Hendrix formed a new group, the Band of Gypsies. They recorded one album in 1970, named after the band, which is a live recording of their debut concert at the Filmore East in New York City on December 31, 1970. Hendrix would record one more album before he died of an accidental drug overdose in 1970 at the age of twenty-seven: the double LP *Electric Ladyland*.

During the five years or so that he was active in the studio, Hendrix experimented with funk, jazz, and Mississippi Delta blues, but never released such an album. From these sessions, producers posthumously culled tracks and released them.

In July of 1995, Al Hendrix, Jimi's father, gained control of his son's estate. With the help of Jimi's sister, Janie Hendrix-Wright, he has brought to fruition a video of the making of *Electric Ladyland*.

Jimi Hendrix is buried in Greenwood Memorial Cemetery in Renton, Washington, a suburb of Seattle.

Frank Zappa (1940–1993)

While Hendrix was arguably the most talented player, Zappa was probably the most sophisticated and imaginative composer of the 1960s rock scene.

Born in Baltimore, Zappa grew up in California. He first started playing drums, and his heightened percussive and rhythmic sense can be heard woven throughout all of his guitar playing. He joined a band called the Soul Giants in 1964. The following year they transformed themselves into the Mothers of Invention, and in 1966 they released their first LP,

Freak Out. The album introduced the intense and emotional world of rock-and-roll to Zappa's sardonic humor, penchant for creating pastiches of popular styles, and avant-garde musical experimentation.

From the start, Zappa tried to expand the musical language of rock by folding in modern classical and jazz-influenced harmony, odd time signatures, exotic instruments, and studio techniques like editing, overdubbing, and tape manipulation. He developed a way of playing the guitar in long, directional solos with effects, expanding organically with his rhythmic and melodic ideas. Zappa created highly innovative material that has both quality and depth.

Robert Fripp (1946–)

Fripp has been in the vanguard of rock music for more than thirty years, exploring the no-man's-land where rock and experimental music meet.

Born in Dorset, England, he began his musical career in the 1960s with the League Of Gentlemen, a group primarily known for backing visiting American pop stars during their visits to the U.K. Later, with brothers Peter and Mike Giles, he formed the trio Giles, Giles and Fripp. They recorded one album, the odd *The Cheerful Insanity of Giles, Giles and Fripp*, in 1968.

Fripp's next band is arguably the most famous of his projects, King Crimson, in which he was joined by Mike Giles. Beginning with their debut album in 1969, *In The Court Of The Crimson King*, the band established themselves as one of the best in progressive rock, combining Hendrix-influenced rock with sophisticated composition and improvisation borrowed from jazz, classical, and experimental music. For five years, King Crimson had numerous personnel changes. Fripp broke up the band in 1974.

After the demise of Crimson, Fripp more fully embraced an on-again, off-again collaboration with former Roxy Music member and synthesizer whiz Brian Eno. Together, they recorded two albums of heavily layered, atmospheric electronic music, *No Pussyfooting* (1973) and *Evening Star* (1975), on which he used a system of endless tape loops dubbed "Frippertronics" to create a harmonically dense thicket of accompaniment. The Frippertronics system became a signature sound on many of Fripp's subsequent solo records and signaled Fripp's presence on records on which he appeared as a guest artist, including albums by David Bowie, Peter Gabriel, and Daryl Hall.

In 1979, Fripp came out with his first solo album, *Exposure*, whose hard edge acknowledged the dawning punk rock movement, but two years later, to everyone's surprise, Fripp reconstituted King Crimson, featuring former bandmate Bill Bruford as drummer as well as newcomers Adrian Belew and Tony Levin. The new lineup recorded three albums—*Discipline*, *Three of A Perfect Pair*, and *Beat*—before disbanding in 1984. For the rest of the decade, Fripp worked on various solo projects, using the name of his first group, The League of Gentlemen, for a series of albums and touring with a traveling guitar workshop, The League of Crafty Guitarists.

For a third time King Crimson became a working band, releasing *Vrooom* (1994) and then *Thrak* (1995). The group remains active, recording and touring. Fripp is also following a parallel career as a solo performer, exploring electronic and experimental music such as the *Soundscape* series of albums in the mid-1990s, and *A Temple in the Clouds* (2000).

Jimmy Page (1944–)

With the formation of Deep Purple and Led Zeppelin in 1968, a style of heavy rock emerged that was a clear synthesis of blues, rock, classical guitar, and jazz, although powered by driving high-powered amplification and effects.

One of the key figures to emerge in this field was Jimmy Page. Born in Heston, England, Page was performing and recording as a teenager in London in the late 1950s and early 1960s. He produced John Mayall's *I'm Your Witchdoctor*, (1965) which featured Eric Clapton, and the next year he joined The Yardbirds. In mid-1968, the quartet split over artistic differences. Page went on to form the New Yardbirds, a hard-rock group that fulfilled the remaining contractual obligations of the Yardbirds.

The New Yardbirds quickly changed their name to Led Zeppelin and became arguably the most popular hard-rock group of the 1970s, selling tens of millions of albums worldwide. Because of the success of Led Zeppelin, Page became widely acknowledged as one of the most talented guitarists in rock music. In addition to his guitar work, Page also produced Led Zeppelin's albums, developing and shaping the band's sound.

The band broke up in the early 1980s, and several years later Page recorded with a new quartet called The Firm, which released two Top 30 albums in 1985 and 1986 before it disbanded. In 1988, Page released his solo debut, *Outrider*, on Geffen Records; the album featured appearances by former Led Zeppelin vocalist Robert Plant and drummer Jason Bonham, the son of Zeppelin drummer John Bonham.

During the 1990s, Page worked with former Whitesnake vocalist David Coverdale, and then reunited with Plant for an *MTV Unplugged* special that showcased the pair performing old Led Zeppelin songs with a world music twist. Some of that material appeared on 1994's *No Quarter*, which was supported by a world tour.

In 1999, he teamed with the Black Crowes for a concert in England that led to a U.S. tour, and an album called *Jimmy Page and the Black Crowes Live at the Greek,* which has exclusive online distribution through Musicmaker.com. Today, Page continues to record and perform.

Jeff Beck (1944–)

Along with Jimi Hendrix and Eric Clapton, Beck is considered one of the great guitarists of his generation, renowned for his technical ability and versatility. Though he has not received the same sort of media attention as Clapton and Hendrix, he nevertheless has hundreds of thousands of fans worldwide.

Born in Wallington, England, Beck attended art school in London but spent most of his time performing with various local bands. A stint with the infamous Screaming Lord Sutch (now a British political figure) built up Beck's reputation to the point where, in 1965, the Yardbirds asked him to replace their departing guitarist, Eric Clapton.

Beck performed with the blues-rock group for about a year and a half, maintaining their hit streak with Top 10 cuts like "Heart Full of Soul," while extending the group's R&B sound to a more Hendrix-like psychedelic territory, such as "Shapes of Things."

By the end of 1966, Beck left the Yardbirds to create the Jeff Beck Group, working with Rod Stewart. They released their debut LP, *Truth,* in 1968, and were one of the first bands to establish the kind of heavy-metal sound that Led Zeppelin developed. In 1970, Rod Stewart and Ron Wood left and joined Small Faces. Beck reformed the Group with vocalist Bobby Tench, bassist Clive Chaman, keyboardist Max Middleton, and drummer Cozy Powell. In 1973 he formed a new trio with former Vanilla Fudge/Cactus members Tim Bogart (bass) and Carmine Appice (drums).

In 1975, Beck made a comeback with the acclaimed *Blow by Blow*, an instrumental jazz fusion album produced by Beatles producer George Martin. For his follow-up album, *Wired*, Beck worked with ex-Mahavishnu Orchestra keyboardist Jan Hammer, repeating the success of *Blow by Blow*.

In 1985, the polished pop-rock album *Flash*, recorded with session musicians, became one of his most commercially successful albums, spawning the hit single "People Get Ready" (sung by Rod Stewart) and the Grammy-winning instrumental "Escape."

After taking some time off and appearing on Mick Jagger's 1987 album *Primitive Cool*, Beck returned with an all-instrumental album, *Guitar Shop*, in 1989. It won a Grammy for Best Rock Instrumental and received widespread critical acclaim. In March 1999, Beck released his first album of original material in more than a decade, *Who Else!*, a collection of eleven new guitar compositions in styles ranging from techno to blues to traditional Irish, arranged and produced by Beck and Tony Hymas. *You Had It Coming* came out in 2001.

CHAPTER 7

How to Find and Buy a Guitar

Finding What's Right for You

Choosing and buying a guitar is a fairly important step in learning how to play. The absolutely best thing you can do is take along a friend or teacher who plays the guitar and have them help you. This won't always be possible, of course, so you're going to have to learn how to find a good guitar for yourself unaided.

In general, don't buy an instrument on your first visit to a music store. Test lots of different types of guitars and visit lots of music stores more than once before you make a decision on your instrument.

Coming up with a plan now that defines your ideas about music doesn't mean you can't change your mind later on. This isn't do or die, here. It's just a place to start. To begin, you'll want to consider issues such as type, expense, appearance, construction, neck, and action, which are covered next.

Types of Guitars

There are three types of guitar to consider: classical; acoustic (and acoustic-electric) steel string; or solid-body electric. What you buy largely depends on the kind of music you like to listen to and want to learn to play.

If you're not sure exactly what you want to learn, or if you want to learn to play a number of styles, you should choose either a classical or a "folk" (acoustic) guitar. A classical guitar uses nylon strings, which are a little easier on your left-hand fingertips (assuming you're right-handed), though the neck is a little broader than a folk guitar. A folk guitar has steel strings, which are a little tougher on your fingertips at first, but it has a narrower neck.

Learning to play an acoustic instrument—"unplugged," in effect—is cheaper and easier than going straight for an electric guitar and amplifier, which could prove to be more expensive and complicated. Once you have some familiarity with the instrument, you'll know better which kind you want to learn to play next.

There are lots of different types of guitars built for the many different kinds of music you can play. If you go into a music store and say you're looking for a guitar to play Eric Clapton–like rock blues, the salesperson will show you a solid-bodied electric like the Fender Stratocaster or a Gibson Les Paul. Say that you want to play jazz guitar like Emily Remler or Johnny Smith, and the salesperson will bring you an F-hole, hollow-bodied cello acoustic guitar like the Gibson ES-175 or a Gibson Super 400.

For blues and R&B, the axe of choice is often a Gibson ES-335, or ES-355. If your passion is folk music and your hero is Jewel, Judy Collins, or early Bob Dylan, go for a Martin or an Ovation. If you want to play classical or flamenco, start on a nylon-string guitar.

The truth is, though, that you can play anything on any kind of guitar. What counts is not the kind of guitar you have, but what's in your head. The best advice is to keep it simple. Remember, even "wild men" like Jimi Hendrix, Chuck Berry, and Steve Vai could play acoustic guitar as well as they could play electric.

Expense

First things first: money. Buying cheap is not necessarily the best idea, though you don't have to spend thousands of dollars on an instrument and equipment, either. Don't put yourself into debt, but be aware that you should think in terms of at least $200 to $300. You could easily spend a $1,000 or more if you're not careful.

The more expensive the guitar is, the better (and more seductive) it seems to be. You need to try to balance the "new toy" syndrome with a realistic understanding of what you can afford, and what you need to learn to play well. Play a really expensive guitar and compare it to a much cheaper model. What differences do you notice?

Unless you are working as a musician and you're buying yourself a new tool of the trade, don't spend too much. It won't be worth it.

Used or Secondhand Instruments

Is it a good idea to buy a used or secondhand guitar? Certainly. While a new guitar has to be broken in and can take up to six months to "wake up," a used guitar in good condition is "alive" and could be a bargain. You can expect to pay as much as 40 percent less than list price for a used guitar (unless it's a classic of some sort), depending on where you get it. Compare the prices in music stores, pawn shops, and newspaper ads, and gather as much knowledge and information as you can.

Mail Order Guitars

Is it a good idea to buy a guitar through a mail order or over the Internet? Not really. Just like buying a car, you need to "test-drive" the instrument, making sure that you're comfortable with it and that it works. Just knowing the make and model isn't a guarantee that a particular instrument is worth buying, or worth the money people are asking for it.

FACTS

Call a music store, or check out catalogs for model prices. A Gibson Les Paul sells for approximately $2,500. A Fender Stratocaster costs around $1,000, and a decent factory-made nylon-string classical guitar can be bought for as little as $300 or so.

Esthetics/Appearance

A blue guitar does not inherently play better than a red or blonde one. Of course, what your new "partner" looks like is important in terms of your desire to spend a lot of time with it. Still, never buy a guitar on looks alone.

Construction

Gently tap the top and back of the instrument to make sure nothing rattles. (You're listening for loose struts inside.) Look inside the sound hole for glue spills and other signs of sloppy workmanship. Check that all the pieces of wood join together smoothly and that there are no gaps between pieces.

An acoustic guitar's sound is principally made by the top—the back and sides reflect and amplify the sound. So a solid-wood acoustic guitar is preferable to a laminated-wood guitar (where the manufacturer presses together layers of inexpensive wood and covers the top layer with veneer). However, solid-wood guitars can be very expensive, and laminated-wood guitars can be pretty good. They are sometimes stronger than solid-wood guitars; the lamination process results in a stronger (though less acoustically responsive) wood.

With electric guitars, make sure that knobs, wires, and other metal parts are secure and rattle-free. Strum the open strings strongly and listen for rattles. A solid-body guitar is basically an electric instrument with no real acoustic sound. The wood that it's made from is irrelevant. It is all electrics. So make sure the pickups and wiring are in good working order. There should be no hum or shorts, and the volume and tone controls should all work without crackles and other noises.

Another important consideration is how long the note will sustain. To check this out you need to use an amplifier for best results. Fret a note and play it. Don't use an open string and don't move the string, just keep fretting the note until it fades away. Why bother with this? Well, a good sustain period is four seconds or more, which means the guitar will be good for playing fusion and rock. It also means the guitar is in good order. If the sustain is less than four seconds, then it's a questionable instrument and you should think twice about buying it. Bear in mind, however, that this doesn't necessarily make it a bad instrument. There could be a number of reasons why the sustain is not longer. If the guitar is otherwise a bargain, this problem might be easily fixed by a guitar repairman. Have a professional check out the instrument before you make a final decision. The lack of sustain could be something as simple as a bridge that is out of alignment, a nut that needs to be filed properly, or just that the strings are old or simply not good.

It might very well be the right thing for a first-time electric guitar buyer to buy a Squier Stratocaster or an Epiphone Les Paul copy instead of the name-brand "real thing." The difference in price is huge—on the order of $300 rather than $1000—and the differences in quality and play are subtle.

Neck

Pick up the guitar by the head and peer down the neck to make sure it's not warped. Does the guitar have a truss rod? Most guitars now come with them, but make sure. Does the neck bolt on? You can usually see where the neck is attached at the heel with a heel plate, under which are four or five bolts. Fender Stratocasters and Telecasters have bolt-on necks. Is the neck glued on? Classical guitars, or the Gibson Les Paul, have glued necks. It looks as though the neck and the body are made from one piece of wood.

Run your fingers along the edge of the neck to make sure the fret wire doesn't need filing or reseating. The fret wire should be seated well on the fingerboard, and the ends should not be loose or feel jagged. Is the neck made from ebony, rosewood, or maple? Cheaper guitars use mahogany or plywood stained black or rust red. The more expensive guitars with the better fingerboards are worth the money. Are the notes at the bottom of the neck in tune? Are they as easy to play as the notes at the top of the fingerboard? Do any of the notes have a buzzing sound even though you're stopping them properly? Is the intonation accurate? Do the notes on the twelfth fret correspond to the harmonics at the same place? The notes may have different tonal qualities, but they should have the pitch. Pay attention to the third and sixth strings in particular. On a guitar that's not set up well, or has a problem, these strings may be hard to keep in tune.

If you don't trust your own knowledge or ears, enlist the help of an experienced guitarist. It's vital to make sure you don't buy something that's going to be really hard to play.

Action

The instrument's "action" or playability is determined by the setting of the string over and between the bridge (at the bottom of the guitar) and the nut (just before the tuning heads). Setting and adjusting these two things is a real art, but the strings shouldn't be so low that the notes buzz when they are played, nor so high that the notes need a lot of physical strength to hold down. If the notes are hard to play or out of tune, get someone in the store to adjust the instrument. If they can't— or won't—fix the instrument, don't buy it.

A Second Guitar

If you're thinking of buying a second guitar, don't go crazy. You should have reached the stage where you realize the limitations of your current instrument, and you should have a much more precise idea of what you want to do with your next axe. In general, go for an instrument that is a little more expensive than the one you have at present, or that gives you more range and flexibility to explore different music sounds and styles, such as a twelve-string or an electric guitar and amplifier.

In the Store

We can practically guarantee that the salesperson's first question for you will be "How much do you want to spend?"

Know the answer. It will save the two of you a lot of time and aggravation. Almost certainly, the next topic of conversation will involve what kind of music you want to play on the instrument (there's no point noodling around on a Fender Stratocaster, and waxing lyrical about Paco Pena and flamenco), and what level of technical accomplishment you've reached on the instrument.

Listen carefully to what the salesperson has to say, and don't be hustled into a sale. After the pitch, say, "Thanks, I'd like to think about it." Then leave the store and at least have a cup of coffee before you decide to return and plunk down your hard-earned cash. Ideally, go to another store and go through the process again. Listen for differences in what the two salespeople have to say to you about the same subjects.

Jack Wilkins's Tips for Buying a Guitar

- Buy quality when possible, but don't overspend.
- Enjoy the instrument. Fall in love, if you can. Finding the right guitar is like meeting the woman (or man) of your dreams. There's an immediate "simpatico" or magnetism that is inexplicable, but nevertheless real.

- Check the fingerboard for warping. Look down the neck as if sighting down a rifle barrel. It's normal to see slight curving around the seventh fret, which can be adjusted using the truss rod, but if the neck looks twisted, don't buy it.
- Check the intonation. The twelfth fret should always be exactly one octave higher than the open string.
- Check the action. Look at the distance between the nut and the bridge. A low action means the strings are closer to the frets, so your fingers don't have to work as hard to press the strings to the fingerboard. Listen for buzzes and rattles.
- Check the tuning heads. If they turn too easily the strings may slip, making the guitar difficult to keep in tune.
- Check the sustain on each note. Sustain is the length of time a note rings out. Play every note on the fretboard to make sure all the notes sustain equally.
- If you're buying an electric guitar, check the pickups. Make sure each string has the same volume level. Significant differences can indicate the pole (or screw beneath each string) may need to be adjusted. If not, the whole pickup may need replacing.
- Check for noise. With the guitar plugged in, stand it close to an amplifier and listen. Whistling or feedback might suggest the pickups aren't well isolated, and it could be a problem playing the guitar at high volume. Make sure the amplifier in the store is not masking faults with the guitar you're playing.

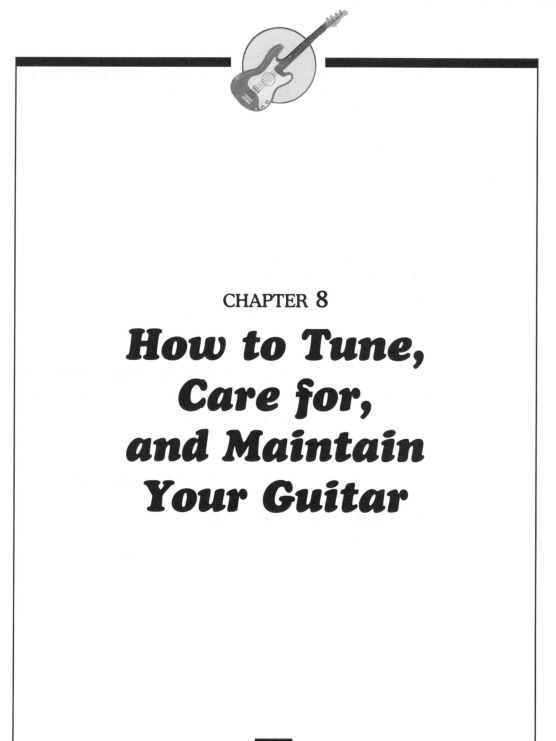

CHAPTER 8

How to Tune, Care for, and Maintain Your Guitar

Anatomy of a Guitar

If you look at **FIGURE 1(a)**, you'll see that a guitar has three basic parts: a body, a neck, and a head.

Body

The body in an acoustic guitar is where the sound comes from. It consists of a top piece, which is a sounding board with a sound hole, and a back and sides, which contain the sound and make it resonate.

In a purely electric guitar, the body is made of a solid piece of wood to avoid "feedback," or too much resonance or screeching when the sound is amplified. It also houses the electronic pickups (which convert the motion of the strings into an electronic signal that can be sent through an amplifier of some kind), and volume and tone controls (which vary the loudness and bass and treble frequencies of the signal). There is also a socket called an *output jack,* into which you insert a special plug or jack. The other end of the jack goes into a corresponding socket in an amplifier.

In addition, the body has a bridge, made from either wood or metal, which anchors the strings. There are also strap pins or posts, which you can use to attach a shoulder strap.

Neck

The neck is usually fixed to the body by bolts or glue, or formed from the body in one piece. It often has a metal truss rod running through it to strengthen it and help adjust any slight warping or twisting. The neck has a flat piece of wood (usually mahogany or ebony) called the *fingerboard* or *fretboard.* The fingerboard is divided into sections called *frets.* These sections are marked off by pieces of wire set into the wood, called *fretwire.* By stopping a string in between the fretwires—that is, "in the middle of the fret"—the frets determine the different pitches or notes you can make on each string. The strings run from the bridge, along the neck and across the nut—which is a piece of wood, plastic, or metal at the top of the neck with slight grooves for each of the six strings—to the tuning pegs.

FIGURE 1(a):
Acoustic guitar

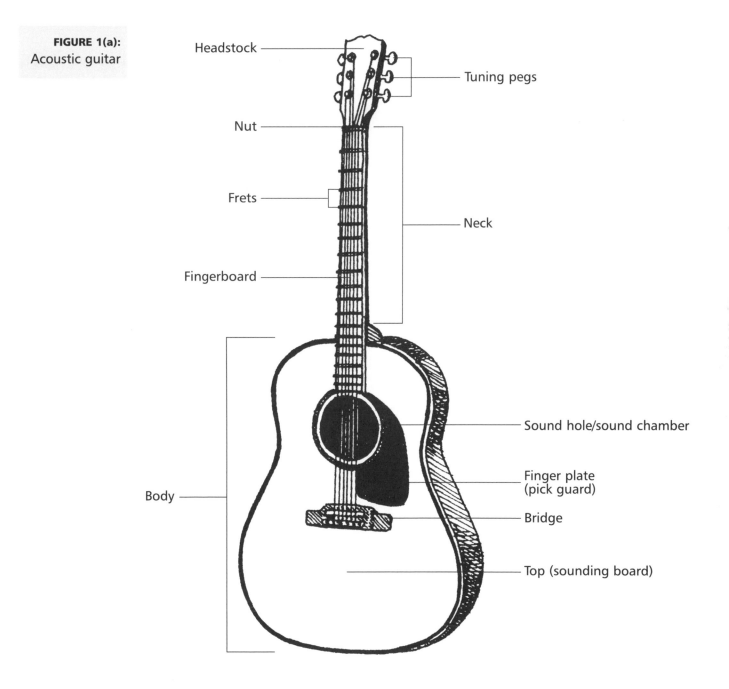

Headstock

Tuning pegs

Nut

Frets

Neck

Fingerboard

Body

Sound hole/sound chamber

Finger plate
(pick guard)

Bridge

Top (sounding board)

FIGURE 1(b):
Electric guitar

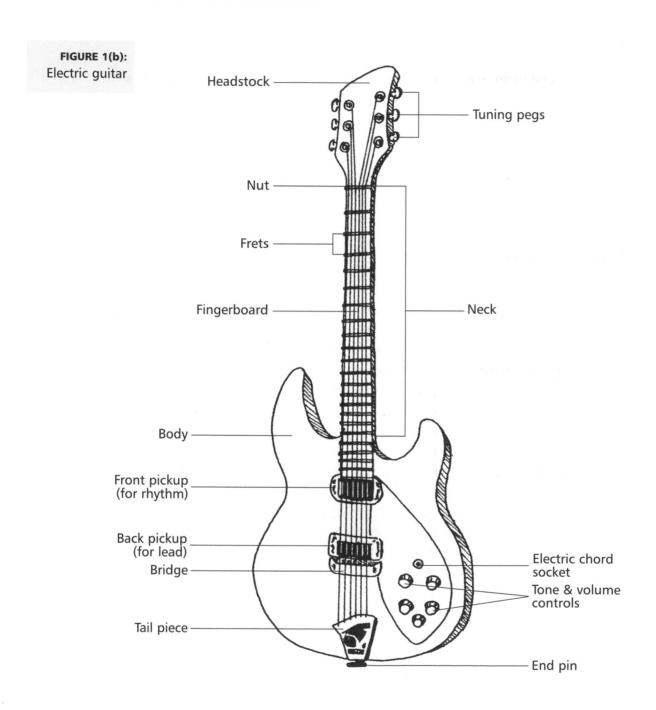

Headstock

Tuning pegs

Nut

Frets

Fingerboard

Neck

Body

Front pickup
(for rhythm)

Back pickup
(for lead)

Bridge

Electric chord
socket

Tone & volume
controls

Tail piece

End pin

Head

The head, sometimes called a *headstock,* holds the tuning pegs (also called *tuning machines, machine heads,* or *tuning gears*) that the strings are attached to. In a six-string guitar there are six tuning pegs. Each tuning peg has a knob you can turn using your fingers. The knob will tighten or loosen the string tension and thus put each string into "tune."

There are three bass strings and three treble strings. (More about strings appears later.)

How It All Works

The principle of the guitar is simple. A string is stretched at high tension across the fingerboard between the tuning peg and either the bridge or the tail piece. By using a fingertip to stop the string at various places on the fingerboard, and plucking the string near the sound hole, you can make the string produce a variety of pitches, or notes. The shorter the length of string, the higher the pitch; the longer the string, the lower the pitch. (That's why a double bass has a booming bass sound, and a mandolin or violin has a more high-pitched treble sound.)

As with string length, string thickness also affects pitch. The thinner the string, the higher the pitch. Besides the length of the string affecting whether you get a high note (short length = treble) or a low note (long length = bass) the strings range in thickness. The thinnest is the E String 1 (treble) and the thickest is the E String 6 (bass). (This is all elementary physics and acoustics if you want to delve into the science of the thing. We won't bother here.) The gauge of a string refers to its thickness. So you can have the same pitch on, say, the E String 1, but use different gauges. Read that again if you need to, to get the idea.

By angling the bridge "just right" you change the string length and therefore help create the right pitch. You add to this by using strings of varying thickness, called gauges which are measured in millimeters.

What's the advantage of having, say, an E String 1 that is a thin gauge? The answer is that the string is more easily bendable and therefore works better for certain types of playing. You don't want heavy gauge strings for rock playing, but rather light gauge. For jazz you would use heavier gauge. For example, Steve Vai probably uses a .009 or .010 String 1 while jazz guitarist Pat Martino might use a .013 or higher on his first string.

ESSENTIALS

The principle of the guitar is simple. A string is stretched at high tension across the fingerboard between the tuning peg and the bridge. By using a fingertip to stop the string at various places on the fingerboard, and plucking the string near the sound hole, you can make the string produce a variety of pitches, or notes.

Each fret on the guitar is a "half-step" away from the fret on either side. A half-step is the smallest interval, or distance between two notes, you can have in Western music. If you look carefully at a piano keyboard, you'll see it's mostly made up of alternating black notes and white notes that are half-steps away from each other.

On the guitar, to play two notes a half-step away from each other, all you have to do is stop any string in the middle of a fret, and then stop that string in the middle of the next fret. So to go up or down the guitar in half-steps, all you have to do is move your finger up or down the strings, stopping the strings one fret at a time.

Electric guitars have added elements. Just like an acoustic guitar, shortening or lengthening a string will give you a variety of pitches, or notes. But there's a problem: Without a hollow body that resonates, where does the sound come from?

The sound comes from electronic pickups, wire-wrapped magnets that act like tiny microphones placed under each string. The vibrations of the string cause the magnet in a pickup to resonate (or more accurately, to "modulate") a tiny magnetic field. That signal is picked up by the pickup and turned into a small electrical current. In turn, that current is conducted from the pickup to an external amplifier by an electrical cord that has one end plugged into the guitar and the other into an amplifier. How loud the note is—and whether it's distorted, or thick and bass-y, or thin and treble-y—is all determined by volume, tone, and effects controls on both the guitar and the amplifier.

Tuning the Guitar

A joke goes that a beginning guitarist spent nearly $3,000 on a new Gibson Les Paul. He proudly went along for his first music lesson, and almost boastfully asked the teacher to try out the guitar, sure that the teacher would praise such an excellent purchase.

Instead, the teacher strummed a few chords, and then said, "It's a bit out of tune. We should have a lesson on how to tune it."

Angrily, the student said, "Are you kidding me? That guitar cost me a fortune. What a ripoff! It was definitely in tune when I bought it in the music store!"

Care and maintenance of your instrument is an important and normal part of learning to play the guitar (or any instrument). Keeping the strings in tune, and even changing them on a regular basis, is important if you want to get the best from your guitar.

Unless you're going to make a habit of treating guitars like Jimi Hendrix or Pete Townsend, who climaxed their stage acts by smashing and burning their instruments (not recommended!), don't drop your new guitar, or scratch it. However, changing strings and tuning your guitar is recommended (highly) if you want to get the most from your axe.

There are lots of ways of tuning your guitar, and lots of types of tunings you can experiment with. However, for the moment we're going to concentrate on only one tuning—the standard "concert" tuning. The thickest bass note is called String 6, and the strings are tuned as follows:

String 6: E

String 5: A

String 4: D

String 3: G

String 2: B

String 1: E

Notice that the top string (1) and the bottom string (6) are the same note, but two octaves apart.

Strings 6, 5, and 4 are the bass strings. Strings 3, 2, and 1 are the treble strings. String 6 is the thickest; String 1 is the thinnest.

Try to memorize the names of the open strings. Once again, they are E, A, D, G, B, and E. Make up a phrase starting with each letter so you can easily recall the string names.

FIGURE 2(a):
Open strings
and notes on
the 5th fret

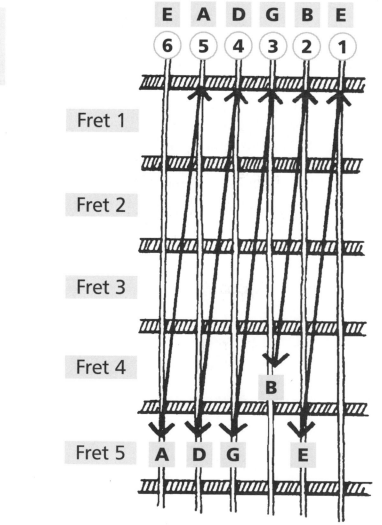

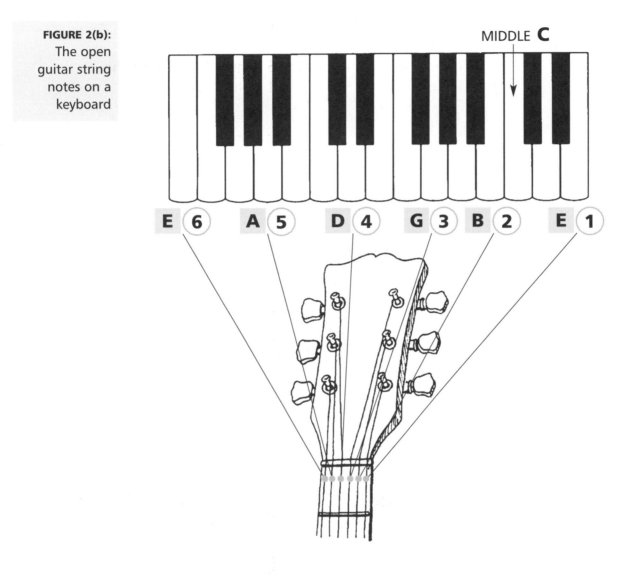

FIGURE 2(b):
The open guitar string notes on a keyboard

MIDDLE **C**

E 6   A 5   D 4   G 3   B 2   E 1

Relative Tuning

The easiest way to tune your guitar if you're playing alone is called *relative tuning*. That means the guitar is in tune relative to itself, although not necessarily to other instruments. You can tune the guitar from any string, but usually you start from String 6, the E bass string.

When you're tuning two strings together, listen for the "wow-wow-wow" pulsing sound that will tell you how close or how far out of tune the string is. What you're aiming for is a perfectly uniform sound of both strings with no "wow-wow" sound at all. The slower that sound is, the closer you are to putting a string in tune. The faster that sound is, the farther away you are from putting the strings in tune.

To begin, count up five frets—that is, five spaces between the fret wires (see **FIGURE 2(a)**)—on String 6. Then use your first fingertip on your left hand to stop the string at this fret and play the note. This is the note A. Now play String 5 while the note on String 6 is still sounding. (Make sure to play String 5 "open," without stopping it at any frets.) Listen for the "wow-wow-wow" sound the two strings make as they sound together. Is the note of String 5 higher or lower than the note of String 6? If it is higher, then you are sharp. Turn the tuning peg on String 5 to lower the sound of the note. If it is higher, then you are flat. Turn the tuning peg until the note sounds higher.

Keep playing both strings at the same time, or one string immediately after the other, so that both notes are sounding at the same time. If you're not sure, keep lowering the note on the open string until it is obviously too low, then try raising it again. The closer you get to being in tune, the more the "wow-wow-wow" sound will slow down and eventually disappear. When it disappears completely, you're in tune. Just get it as close as you can for the moment.

Next, stop String 5 at the fifth fret and play the note there. (The note is D.) Play String 4 open at the same time. Again, adjust the open string using the tuning peg until both strings are sounding the same note.

Next, stop String 4 at the fifth fret and play the note there (G). Play String 3 open at the same time. Again, adjust the open string using the tuning peg until both strings are sounding the same note.

Notice that tuning String 2 is slightly different. Stop String 3 at the fourth fret and play the note there (B). Play String 2 open at the same time. Again, adjust the open string using the tuning peg until both strings are sounding the same note.

Next, stop String 2 at the fifth fret and play the note there (E). Play String 1 open at the same time. Again, adjust the open string using the tuning peg until both strings are sounding the same note.

If the strings are new, they may slip a little bit. Tuning is about constant adjustment. So don't be afraid to go back and try to adjust the strings already in tune to make sure they haven't gone out of tune a little bit.

Other Ways to Tune a Guitar

Here are some other things you can do to make sure the strings are in tune with each other:

Play String 1 and String 6 together. They're both E strings, remember (though two octaves apart). Try to make sure they sound the same note.

Play notes an octave apart. To do this, stop String 5 at the seventh fret. This sounds the note E. Now play String 6 (E) open at the same time. Make the adjustment to the higher-pitched, fretted string. The two notes are an octave apart. Do the same on the other strings. Remember, on String 3 stop the string at the eighth fret and play String 2 open to sound the note B. Then play the String 2 at the seventh fret and String 1 open.

Match octaves by playing every other string. Again, make the adjustment to the higher-pitched, fretted string. Play String 6 (E) open, then stop String 4 at the second fret (E) and sound that note at the same time. Then match String 5 (A) open with String 3 stopped at the second fret. Play String 4 (D) open, with String 2 stopped at the third fret. Play String 3 (G) open with String 1 stopped at the third fret.

ESSENTIALS   Get into the habit of making sure your guitar is in tune every time you pick it up to play.

Tuning Using Harmonics

This is a complicated subject. For now, just accept the following. If you lightly touch a string over the fret wire on the twelfth fret with a finger while gently plucking close to the bridge, you will get a note called a *harmonic*.

Following the same "light touch" technique, play the harmonic on String 6 at the fifth fret (E), followed by the harmonic on String 5 at the seventh fret. Adjust String 5 until it's in tune.

Compare harmonics on String 5, fifth fret (A), and then String 4, seventh fret. Adjust String 4 if necessary.

Compare harmonics on String 4, fifth fret (D) with String 3, seventh fret. Adjust String 3.

Compare harmonics on String 6, seventh fret (B) with String 2, twelfth fret. Adjust String 2.

Compare harmonics on String 5, seventh fret (E) with String 1, twelfth fret. Adjust String 1.

Strum a chord, such as G, A minor, or E, one string at a time (arpeggio style), and then together, and listen to the strings working in harmony with each other. Bear in mind that a string may sound out of tune in one chord, and work well in another.

Tuning takes practice and patience, but it's important that you master it.

Tuning to a Reference Source

We've looked at tuning the guitar to itself, but what do you do if you're playing with other musicians and your guitar is out of tune with them? Well, you tune to a fixed source. You can use pitch pipes, a tuning fork, a piano, another guitar, or an electronic tuning box that will help you put each string into "concert" pitch. (This is the term for commonly accepted pitches that everyone uses, regardless of their instrument.) You can even find music software programs (some of them are free or share-ware on the Web) that will give you the correct pitch for your strings.

A tuning fork will be tuned to concert A, below middle C. Strike the fork until it hums, then place the leg of the fork against the body of the guitar near the bridge so you can hear it resonate. Then, while the fork is sounding, play String 5 open (A) and listen for the pulsing until the string is in tune.

Strings

Strings don't last forever. In fact, depending how much you play and practice, and whether you live in a hot climate or not, you could change your strings as often as once a week. In general, however, once every eight to twelve weeks is about average. If a string breaks, it's probably time to change the whole set, rather than just replace the one that broke. Strings lose their stretch and vibrancy over time because of salt from sweaty fingers and rust. You can also find a variety of problems with bridges and nuts, and so forth, which we'll get into later on.

You can extend the life of your strings by cleaning them after each session. To get rid of the grunge under the string, some players "snap" each string by pulling it back slightly, as if the string is on a bow, and then snapping it back to the fingerboard.

Here's a trick used by string bass players: Take off the strings and boil them in water for ten minutes or so. This removes grease and grunge. However, replacing treble strings in particular can be a pain. Better to just bite the bullet and get a new set of strings.

Strings come in a variety of gauges. The thicknesses are described in fractions of an inch. Choosing a gauge of string is very much a personal decision.

In general, the lighter the string gauge the easier it is to bend and hold down the strings for lead playing. The thicker the gauge, the better the volume, the longer the sustain, and the easier it is to keep the guitar in tune. A thicker gauge is also easier for rhythm playing. The common gauges are:

Ultra-light:	.008 (String 1) to .038 (String 6)
Extra-light:	.010 (String 1) to .050 (String 6)
Light:	.011 (String 1) to .052 (String 6)
Medium:	.013 (String 1) to .056 (String 6)
Heavy:	.014 (String 1) to .060 (String 6)

Strings come in three different types: nylon, usually for Spanish or classical-style guitars; bronze, used for acoustic steel-strung instruments because they have little electrical quality; and steel strings, used for electric and acoustic instruments. You should never put steel or bronze strings on guitars that use nylon strings. It will ruin them quickly.

With the exception of Strings 1 and 2 (and sometimes also 3), which are plain metal, steel strings are made up of a thread or core of wire around which another piece of wire is tightly wound. There are three types of winding:

- Flatwound. Most commonly used on archtop guitars, a flat ribbon of steel is wound around a core of wire. Flatwound strings don't "squeak" the way other strings can when you move your fingers along them, but they can produce a somewhat duller tone and are more likely to crack.
- Roundwound. Most electric steel strings are roundwound, a piece of steel that is wound around a steel core. They have a brighter tone than flatwound, and often last longer, but seem a little tougher to play at first.
- Groundwound. These are conventional roundwound strings that have been ground down to create a partially flat surface.

Changing Strings

Guitars are pretty rugged instruments, and changing strings regularly will improve the guitar's sound, help prevent strings breaking at the wrong moment, and help identify possible maintenance problems. (You may discover a rattling tuning peg, or a gouged bridge or nut.) Old strings tend to sound dull and lifeless, and become brittle with age. This makes them feel tougher to fret and harder to keep in tune.

Removing the Old Strings

An old wives tale has it that replacing strings one at a time is better for the guitar because it maintains tension on the neck. Not true. Guitars are made of sterner stuff. However, replacing strings one at a time can be more convenient.

A potential problem with taking all the strings off at the same time is that on guitars with a movable bridge, the bridge *will move.* This isn't something you want to have happen, because resituating a bridge can be a pain. And if the bridge is not positioned properly, it can effect the tuning of the strings and the feel of the neck as you play. A good compromise is to replace the strings three at a time. Replace the bass strings first, putting them in rough tune with the old treble strings, and then replace the treble strings, putting them in tune with the new bass strings. Then you can adjust the tuning of all six new strings.

ESSENTIALS

It can be tedious to turn your tuning pegs. Save yourself time by buying a string winder, which fits over the tuning peg and allows you to turn it far more quickly.

You can just unwind the strings by lessening the tension using the tuning peg, or you can try a more radical approach and use wire cutters to snip the strings near the tuning peg. Once the old strings are off the guitar, throw them away.

Classical Guitars

Classical guitars have fixed bridges, so you can replace the strings all at once if you like. Nylon isn't as springy as steel, but attaching the string to the bridge can be tricky at first.

FIGURE 3(a):
Attaching nylon strings to a bridge

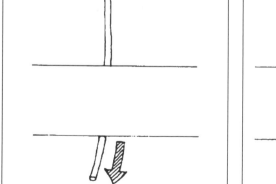
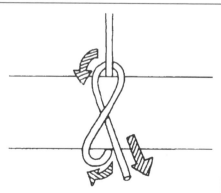

FIGURE 3(b):
Nylon strings
attached to
a bridge

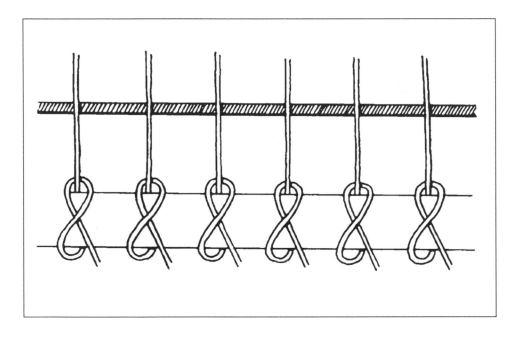

FIGURE 4(a):
Attaching
strings to a
tuning peg

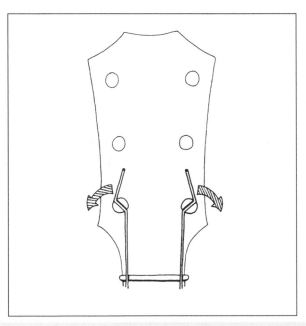

The arrow indicates the direction to turn the tuning peg.

FIGURE 4(b):
Order of strings
as they are
attached to the
tuning pegs

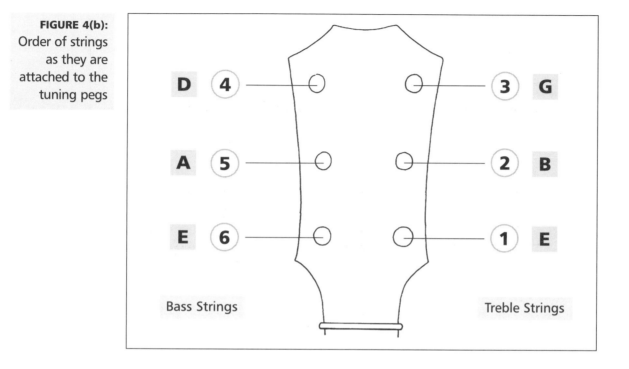

Pass the string through the hole in the bridge, leaving about an inch and a half sticking out the back. Loop the short end back up, and wrap it behind the long end and then under itself. Pull it taut by tugging on the long end of the string. You may have to practice this a few times. Don't cut the string until everything is in place and in tune.

Thread the long end through the hole in the tuning peg at the head. (**FIGURE 4(b)** shows the order of the strings on the head.) Bring the end of the string over the roller (or capstan) in front of the hole and under itself. Make sure the string sits in the small groove on the nut. Then take up some of the slack of the string and tighten the tuning peg by winding the bass strings from right to left (counterclockwise), and treble strings from left to right (clockwise). As it picks up the slack of the string, the tuning peg will tighten and lock itself in place. While the string tightens, start tuning it and stretching it by pulling on it at various times. Once the guitar string is in place and in tune, snip away the excess string, leaving maybe a couple of inches at the tuning peg, and an inch or less at the bridge.

Steel-Strung Acoustic Guitars

Steel-strung acoustic and electric guitars have a moveable bridge, so when you change the strings you want to be careful not to dislodge it. It's a good idea to change the strings one at a time, or three at a time, but not all at the same time in order to keep the bridge anchored in its best position.

Acoustic guitars often have bridges that anchor the end of the string by popping the string into a hole and keeping it in place with a pin. First, loosen the string by slackening off the tension at the tuning peg. Then ease out the bridge pin.

Bridge pins can stick sometimes, so carefully use needle-nose pliers or the blunt edge of a table knife to ease the pin out of its hole. Be careful not to dig into the wood. Once the pin is out, you can remove the string.

Stuff the end of the new string that has a little brass ring into the bridge pin hole. Then wedge the bridge pin back into the hole, locking the ring and the string in place. You'll notice that the pin has a slot. Make sure the slot faces forward (i.e., toward the tuning pegs).

Now pass the string over the bridge post, making sure each string fits snugly into the groove on the bridge and on the nut. Thread the loose end through the hole in the tuning peg post. If you want, you can kink the string a little to help keep it in place. Take up the slack on the string and then turn the tuning peg clockwise for the treble strings, and counterclockwise for the bass strings, tuning the string as the tension increases.

After all the strings are attached, retune the guitar carefully, bringing all the strings up to concert pitch. Be careful; you don't want to break a string. The best technique is to turn the tuning peg a couple of times, then check the tuning until you get the string in tune. When the string is in tune, clip the end off at the tuning peg, leaving about an inch of extra wire protruding.

ESSENTIALS New strings need to be constantly checked, and then "played in" before they settle into the correct tuning.

Electric Guitars

With electric guitars, the string is attached to the bridge by passing one end through a hole and threading the string up to the brass ball, which keeps it in place.

Some guitars use what is called a *locking nut system,* such as a Floyd Rose tremolo unit. These can be a pain to change. The strings are clamped into place at the bridge saddle using a special Allen key. It's a good idea to use a piece of wood or a pack of playing cards to take up the tension when a string is changed; this stops the unit from rocking back and forth. On tremolo units, when one string is changed, the tension on all the strings changes.

In order to use these bridges, you must snip off the ball so that the string can be fitted into a small vise-like mechanism that holds the string in place. When all the strings are changed, you can remove the wood or playing cards supporting the bridge. Tune the strings as usual, using the tuning pegs. Then make the final adjustment on the bridge anchor using an Allen key. But be careful. Don't overtighten the strings at the bridge too soon. If you overtighten a string, when you remove the block supporting the unit, the string may snap as the tension increases.

Remember, if you have a guitar with this kind of bridge, the spare strings need to have the ball ends removed. Get in the habit of carrying wire cutters around in your guitar case.

Basic Repairs and Maintenance

The simplest thing to do to maintain your guitar is clean it. If dust gathers under the head and bridge, dust them off by using a cloth or feather duster, which can clean without the danger of scratching.

Natural oils from your fingers coat the strings every time you play. Over time the strings start to corrode, and not only can it damage the strings' ability to sound good, it can eventually injure the wood of the instrument, seeping into the fingerboard. Wipe down the guitar after every playing session and before you put the guitar back in its case—front, sides, back, fingerboard, and back of the neck as well. A chamois leather cloth is a good investment because it not only cleans but polishes at the same time.

Use a cloth to clean each string. Hold the cloth between your thumb and index fingers, and then run them along the length of each string.

If the guitar has not been used for a while, first dust it and then rub down the wood with furniture polish or, better yet, guitar polish. (Some types of furniture polish contain abrasives that can damage the guitar's finish.) Never put polish directly onto the instrument; it can damage the finish. Put your cleaning solution onto a cloth first.

For the metal parts, you may want to use a mild jewelers' or chrome polish, so long as it's not abrasive.

Be careful! Don't ever touch the pickups of an electric guitar with anything besides a dry brush or cloth. Pickups are electrical, and liquid can cause a short-circuit. Avoid keeping your guitar in a place that's subjected to direct sunlight for long periods of time, or drastic changes in temperature and humidity. This will help keep the guitar surface from cracking. If you do accidentally chip the surface, take the guitar to a professional guitar repairperson, who will easily fix the problem. If you decide to do it yourself, bear in mind that when you add or remove varnish, it can drastically change the wood's ability to vibrate, and thus the guitar's sound.

When traveling, keep the guitar inside the vehicle if you can. A guitar in the trunk, or luggage compartment, can be subjected to extremes of heat and cold. If you have to put it in the trunk, try to put it as close to the passenger compartment as possible, so if you're hit from behind, it stands a chance of surviving the accident.

Also, when traveling, carry your guitar in a hard case. If you're just going to a gig and back, then a good padded nylon gig bag will offer some protection, but not much.

ESSENTIALS

If you're going to travel with your guitar, invest in a hard case to protect it.

If your guitar has been subjected to extreme cold, when you bring it indoors, leave it in its case until it has had time to adjust to the room temperature. Remember, wood expands and contracts, and if it does so too rapidly, your instrument could get damaged. A good rule of thumb for storing your guitar: If you are comfortable in the room, the guitar will be as well.

Alterations and Setting Up the Guitar

Don't fiddle with these things until you're comfortable with the idea that you know what you're doing, and why you're doing it. In most cases, if you're consistently unhappy with how your instrument plays or sounds, you'll be better off taking your guitar to a repair professional, who may even be able to fix these things while you wait. Professional repairpeople often spend time watching the musician play and talking about what the guitarist thinks is right or wrong about the instrument before deciding the best way to set up the guitar.

ESSENTIALS

Fret wire can wear out, and grooves will appear where the strings have worn away the nickel. Eventually the frets will start to buzz. Take your guitar to a professional repairperson, who will replace the fret wire with the best gauge of fret wire for your guitar. A "fret job" can add a new lease of life to an old guitar.

Adjusting the Bridge

By adjusting the bridge you can alter the action of your guitar. The action describes the height of the strings above the fingerboard. The higher the action, the more strength you need to use to fret a note. It can be useful for rhythm playing, when you are principally playing chords all the time. Blues players who use "slides" often use a high action so the "bottleneck" doesn't scrape against the frets.

The lower the action, the easier it is to fret the note. This can be useful for fast, single-note lead guitar playing.

Ideally, you want to set the action as low as you can without getting fret buzzing. This is really a trial-and-error process. (Bear in mind that the thickness of the gauge of string you use can make a difference to playability as well.) Before you make any adjustments to the action, make sure you are using a new set of strings. Old strings can affect the action and intonation.

On most electric guitars, each string has an adjustable saddle on the bridge. Either the saddle will have a screw that will adjust the whole bridge saddle at one go, or each string will have an individual screw that can be raised or lowered. Sometimes it's necessary to adjust the whole bridge saddle by filing it down. This should not be done by anyone except a professional repairperson.

By changing the action, you are also affecting the intonation of the guitar. When you raise or lower the action, you alter the tension and distance between the bridge and the nut. This affects the way the strings play in tune. The distance between the nut and the twelfth fret must be *identical* to the distance between the twelfth fret and the bridge saddle. If it isn't, the guitar won't play in tune. The easiest way to test this is to play the string open, and then play the note at the twelfth fret, or the harmonic at the twelfth fret. It should be identical, though an octave higher. If the note at the twelfth fret is sharp, the string is too short and must be lengthened by moving back the saddle. If the note is flat, then move the saddle toward the nut.

Adjusting the Neck

Temperature changes, humidity, and age can cause guitars to swell and contract. This in turn can affect the setup of the guitar. For example, a slight bow in the neck can cause fret buzz, or difficulty getting a clean note at a particular fret or series of frets. You can sometimes adjust the neck by manipulating the truss rod. The truss rod runs down the center of the neck just under the fingerboard. Not all guitars have them, and even some that do won't allow you to adjust them. Usually you can see whether the truss rod can be adjusted because there is a plate at the headstock near the nut. Once removed, you will see a rod (or sometimes two) that has an adjustable screw or nut end. If you have a new guitar, it probably came with a truss rod wrench.

If your guitar bows out between the seventh and twelfth frets, you'll see a large gap between the strings and fretboard that makes playing the string at this point very hard. Tighten the truss rod, as you face it, by turning the nut a quarter turn clockwise. Give the instrument a few moments after each turn to settle into its new position.

If the frets buzz and the neck bows inward at the same place, you can loosen the truss rod by turning the nut a quarter turn at a time counterclockwise (as you face the guitar). Again allow the instrument to settle after each quarter-turn adjustment.

If you can't fix the problem within a few turns, stop. Overtightening or overloosening the truss rod can ruin a guitar and make it permanently unplayable.

Loose Connections

If you hear a rattle, try strumming the instrument and touching various potential culprits with your free hand until you touch the correct object and the rattling stops. For example, it could be a loose screw in a tuning peg or a loose nut on a jack socket. It's a good idea to gather a small toolkit of screwdrivers, pliers, wrenches, and such that will fit the various sizes of screws and nuts on your guitar.

Tuning Pegs

Tuning pegs, tuning machines, or machine heads (different names for the same thing) are easily replaced if gears get worn or a part breaks off. If more than one tuning peg is giving you trouble, it's probably a good idea to replace the whole set.

The tuning pegs screw into the wood of the head, so take off the string, unscrew the tuning peg, take the peg to a guitar store, and try to get a matching peg. Then screw the new peg into place in the same position as before.

Strap Pins

These are little buttons that you use to attach a strap to the guitar. They usually have regular screw bodies, and they can sometimes work themselves loose. If tightening the pin with a screwdriver doesn't work, dab a little plastic wood or carpenter's glue on the end and put it back. If you still have trouble, go to a professional.

Electrical Problems

Dust and other grunge can affect the electrics of your guitar. If your volume or tone controls start to crackle when you turn them, or you're getting a weak or inconsistent signal, you may have dust or something else on the control. Turn the knobs vigorously back and forth to see if you can work out the dirt. If that doesn't work, try spraying the controls inside with aimed blasts from a can of air. If all else fails, go to a professional, who will give your controls a thorough cleaning.

The crackle can also indicate a loose wire in the jack plug. Take off the jack plate and look for the loose connection. If you spot it, use a soldering iron to reattach the wire to its appropriate lug. If you're uncomfortable doing this, take it to a professional.

Replacing a pickup is not that difficult. Often the pickups that came with your guitar aren't as good as ones you could buy to replace them. Make sure you get a pickup that's the same size and type as the one you're replacing so it fits into the existing holes drilled into the body.

Make sure you know which wire is supposed to be soldered to which connection. Then seat the pickup in the cavity left by the old pickup, and screw it into place. Again, don't attempt this if you don't feel confident you can do the job.

CHAPTER 9

How to Get a Good Sound

Sound Is Personal

Once you reach a comfort level with strumming, playing chords, and single-note playing, you should start to think about the kind of sound you want to get out of your instrument.

Sound is a mental thing. Two guitarists can sit down and use the same amp and guitar (and sometimes even the same acoustic instrument) and produce different sounds that identify the players, much as their voices identify them.

It's how you hear the sound that's important. Musicians of all instruments spend a lot of time experimenting and working on getting not just a good sound, but an individualistic sound. Who are your favorite players? Do you like their sound? Have you tried to re-create it? Investigated how they came up with their sound? In guitar magazines or interviews you can read how players used this guitar with that amp combined with that effect, but somehow when you try using the same setup, it doesn't sound the same. The reason? The sound was in their head and was developed from listening to other guitarists or other instrumentalists they admired, and years of experimentation.

Acoustic Guitars

For acoustic players, getting a good sound means fretting the note cleanly, so that it sounds loud and clear, and sustains well. (Saxophone players practice getting a good sound by playing one note and holding it for a long time, then moving to the next.)

The keys to a good sound are deliberateness—that is, you mean to sound the note and commit to sounding it—and clean articulation. A great way to practice getting a clean sound is to play your scales very slowly and deliberately (there's that word again). Articulate each note of the scale as you fret it.

Electric Guitars

It's possible to play an electric guitar without an amplifier, but unless your guitar is a semi-acoustic or an archtop, the sound will be pretty dismal—rather like flies buzzing around your head, and about as loud.

After you've spent most (but not all, we hope) of your money on your guitar, it's time to consider getting an amplifier. A good guitar and a decent amp will go a long way to helping you create a good sound.

The History of Amplifiers

By 1930, anyone familiar with electricity knew that metal, moving through a magnetic field, caused a disturbance that could be translated into an electric current by a nearby coil of wire. Electrical generators and phonograph (record player) pickups already used this principle. The problem building a guitar pickup was creating a practical way of turning a string's vibration into a current.

After months of trial and error, Hawaiian steel-guitar player George Beauchamp—who, with Adolph Rickenbacker, formed the Electro String Company in the early 1930s—developed a pickup that consisted of two horseshoe magnets. The strings passed through these and over a coil, which had six pole pieces concentrating the magnetic field under each string.

When the pickup seemed to work, Beauchamp enlisted Harry Watson, a skilled guitar maker for National Guitars, to make an electric Hawaiian guitar. It was nicknamed the "Frying Pan."

Electro String had to overcome several obstacles, however. To begin with, 1931 was the worst year of the Great Depression, and no one had money to spend on newfangled guitars. Furthermore, only the most farsighted of musicians saw the potential, and the Patent Office did not know if the Frying Pan was an electrical device or a musical instrument.

From the very beginning, Electro String developed and sold amplifiers. Obvious really, because without an amplifier the new electric guitar would have been useless. The first production-model amp was designed and built by a Mr. Van Nest at his Los Angeles radio shop.

Soon after, Beauchamp and Rickenbacker hired design engineer Ralph Robertson to work on amplifiers. He developed the new circuitry for a line that by 1941 included at least four models. Early Rickenbacker amps influenced, among others, Leo Fender, who by the early 1940s was repairing them at his radio shop in nearby Fullerton, California.

By today's standards, the amps were pretty meek. Their output was about 10 watts, which is pretty low, and they used radio technology, vacuum tubes, and small loudspeakers. However, as the popularity of the electric guitar grew, there was a corresponding demand for louder amps.

The breach was filled by Leo Fender. In 1949 he worked with his engineer, Don Randall, to produce the first Super Amp model amplifier. With the Fender solid-bodied guitars (the Telecaster and Stratocaster) in general production, and the introduction of the Gibson Les Paul in 1952, the demand for amps went through the roof as the popularity of the solid body grew. Output rose to a reasonable 50 watts, with 12-inch speakers, still the norm for guitar amps.

By the late 1950s, the British company Vox had produced the AC30, which is as much a classic amp today as the Fender Twin Reverb. The Vox was particularly popular with blues and rock musicians because it produced a warm tone, which musicians such as Jimi Hendrix, Jeff Beck, and other heavy-metal rockers discovered could be overdriven to create the fuzzy, distorted effect that has come to define the early 1960s rock guitar sound.

Splitting up a combo amp into individual components came about during the rock era of the 1960s. The amp became known as the *head,* and the speakers became known as *the stack*. You could get more powerful amps and much bigger speakers this way, and by combining various amps and speaker combinations, musicians could produce more volume.

As the 1960s wore on, and rock bands played bigger and bigger venues, power and volume once more became a problem. This was solved when the British engineer Jim Marshall produced a 100-watt amp connected to a stack of four 12-inch speakers. Pretty soon the Marshall stack was the norm for rock concerts.

By the 1970s, the vacuum-tube technology of the 1930s was finally being replaced by cheaper and more predictable solid state transistors, although musicians complained about the coldness of the sound, as compared to the warmth of the tube amp. It was popular among those who liked a thinner, cleaner sound.

The brittle sound was offset by the wider frequency range and the ability to play cleanly (without distorting) at higher volumes. Different tubes could produce different sounds, but they needed to be replaced periodically because they came loose, or burned out.

By the 1980s, amplifier makers went back to creating a valve sound, often creating hybrid models that featured tube pre-amps and solid-state power amplifiers, getting the best of both worlds. Today, a traditional guitar amp combines an amplifier and a loudspeaker in one unit, called a *combo*. They are compact and relatively easy to transport.

How Amps Work

Combo amps (and amps in general) come in a variety of sizes and shapes, but there are certain common functions that are on most models. These are input sockets, individual channel volume controls, and tone controls, plus a master volume control.

There are two basic stages in producing a sound through a combo amp: the *pre-amp,* which controls the input volume and tone, and the *power amp*, which controls the overall volume. Most of the tone colors are created during the pre-amp stage.

The input socket takes the signal from the guitar, through the cord that connects the guitar to the amp via a jack socket. If there is more than one input socket, other instruments, such as a second guitar, or a microphone can be fed into the amp at the same time through these other input sockets.

Channel input volume controls allows the player to adjust the volume on the amp. It usually boosts the signal from the guitar and passes that signal along to the tone controls.

Channel tone controls can often be as simple as bass and treble controls. More sophisticated models such as the Mesa Boogie can feature a full-blown graphic equalizer. Basically, the controls split the sound into two or more bands, allowing for precise programming of the sound.

Output volume is the final stage of the process. The signal from the pre-amp passes through the power amplifier and is controlled by a master volume knob that controls the signal to the loudspeaker. The master volume controls the volume of the total output to the speaker, regardless of how many input channels are being used.

Other Controls

More sophisticated models have controls that affect distortion, reverb, and tremolo. Speakers come in a wide range of sizes and can be linked together to produce different kinds and volume of sound. Basically, a loudspeaker is the opposite of a microphone. When a string creates a disturbance in the magnetic field around the pickup, the final adjusted signal (having passed through pre-amp and power amp) is passed to a voice coil, connected to a large diaphragm, often made out of cardboard or some other responsive and flexible material. The coil receives the signal, transmutes that into a magnetic field of its own, and causes the diaphragm and cone to vibrate. The vibration disturbs the surrounding air, and re-creates the sound waves that were originally generated by striking the guitar string.

Most guitar amp loudspeakers are rated by their impedance factor, which varies from 8 ohms to 16 ohms. (*Impedance* is an electrical term. Measured in ohms, it is the total opposition to the flow of the alternating current in a circuit, but don't worry if this makes no sense to you.) It's important that amp output and speaker impedance are matched up. Too high a rating and the overall volume of the combo will be reduced. Standard 12-inch speakers (though 10-inch and 15-inch are also common now) can be connected together in pairs or quads, although the way they are connected will affect the overall sound output.

Getting Started

It's a good idea to begin with a small practice amp that can deliver a good signal at 6 or 12 watts. In general, what you pay for in an amp is power, not features, so practice amps can be quite cheap, less than $100.

It's also worth bearing in mind that you can often plug your guitar into the auxiliary or tape jack of a home stereo unit. If the unit doesn't have a suitable jack plug socket, go to a local electronics store and tell the salespeople what you want to do. They can usually find you an adapter plug that will allow you to plug the guitar jack into a phono plug that will work on the stereo unit.

Before you plug in, however, make sure the volume is way down on the stereo unit, or you'll risk blowing out the speakers. You can even connect small practice amps, with no speakers, to headphones. That way, you can get a range of effects—such as distortion, EQs, and compression—without disturbing anyone else.

Effects

Electronic effects allow you to produce quite a range of tones and colors. Some new combo amps have effects built into them, but most of the time nearly all of the effects you want to produce will have to be created by interposing an effects unit of some sort between the guitar and the amp. The jack plug that would normally be inserted into the amp is inserted in the *in* socket of the effects unit, and another chord connects the *out* socket of the effects unit to the amp. Most effects units are powered by 9-volt batteries, although they also have a wall-socket transformer. A transformer that's not created for the unit can hum, damage the foot pedal, or not even work.

Reverb

This is a natural effect that gives the impression that the sound is bouncing off walls and ceilings. Modern units allow you to program the parameters of the sound, such as the size and shape of the imaginary room. *Reverb* is often used to breathe life into dead sound and is perhaps the most common effect used in a recording studio.

Delay

Like reverb, *delay* gives the sense of sound bounced off a faraway object. You can create different effects depending on the length of the delay, which is measured in milliseconds. (500 milliseconds = half a second.)

Echo

When the delay is long enough that the repeated signal can be heard as a distinct sound in its own right, then you have an *echo*. You can control the speed of the echo and get sounds that range from the early days of 1950s rock-and-roll to the experiments of Robert Fripp, or Queen's Brian May.

Phase and Flange

Phasing takes place when the same signal sounds as though it is being played back from two different sources at the same time. When the two signals are slightly out of sync—that is, when the peaks of the soundwave of one signal are overlayed on the valleys of the second signal—you get a sweeping sound called *phase cancellation* that sounds a little like a revolving Leslie speaker for a Hammond organ, popular in the 1970s. If the delay is more dramatic, then the sweeping sound becomes known as *flanging*.

Chorus

By adding variations in pitch to a delayed signal, it's possible to create the sound of a doubled signal, as if a six-string guitar has become a twelve-string, in a crude analogy.

Pitch Shifting

The signal is digitally sampled—that is, a "piece" of a recorded track is digitally copied and then fed into a loop to be played endlessly. Then it is replayed at a different speed, which changes the original pitch to a new pitch. Units often have a range of an octave above and an octave below the original note. If, for example, you set the unit to play sixths, then every sound that goes into the unit will be played a major sixth higher.

Distortion

The most well-known of all effects, *distorted sound* can be created in a number of different ways. The volume of the signal is boosted to the point of distortion in a pre-amp, and then that distorted signal is amplified by the power amp.

Compression

Often used in conjunction with other effects, *compression* makes the guitar notes sustain for a longer period, giving them more body, although it smoothes out the overall dynamics of a note.

Wah-Wah

Wah-wah is a sound from the 1960s and 1970s, popularized by Frank Zappa and Jimi Hendrix. A foot pedal controls a filter similar to a guitar's tone control, causing an almost vocal-like quality on occasion. The rhythm guitar sound in the original version of the movie *Shaft*, for instance, is a typical wah-wah funk sound.

Tremolo

This is another effect that has a dated 1950s retro sound. Solid-body guitars used to have tremolo arms that could be manually activated. Now it primarily comes in a pedal unit, and it sounds as though you're playing through a slowly moving fan. However, tremolo arms are standard equipment on Fender Stratocasters even today.

Volume Pedal

This is a pedal that can be set so that you can alternate, at the dip of a switch, between playing lead guitar and rhythm guitar. The pedal instantly raises or lowers the volume of the amplifier.

Combining Effects

Effects pedals can be combined, linking them together. However, the exact sequence of effects used can change the sound, depending on whether a particular effect is placed before or after another. If you use more than one effect, it's probably worthwhile considering buying a switching foot pedal unit that will help you control which effect you want to have dominate your sound, and in what order you want the effects to be.

A modern solution to this problem has been the development of a multiple-effects pedal, which can be programmed to remember a particular sound, or sequence of sounds, and also does away with a suitcase full of effects pedals littering the floor before you like mouse traps.

A word of caution: Effects will not make you play better, or help you disguise mistakes. If you can't play well acoustically, you won't play better with a bunch of tricks loaded onto your guitar.

Choose your effects with some taste. They can date you, and they can interfere with the tracking of the guitar signal, making it seem as though you are constantly playing out of sequence—that is, with "bad" time—from the other members of the group.

Always carry a good supply of batteries if you don't have a transformer, and really practice with the effect at home before you decide to use it on a gig or recording.

Jack Wilkins's Tips for Buying an Amp

- Think about what you want the amp for. You're paying for power, mostly, so do you really need that 100-watt monster? Could you get way with a 50-watt combo instead? Or maybe even a practice amp until you start gigging?
- Size is important. Imagine yourself lugging your guitar and amp from gig to gig, going up and down narrow staircases, onto high stages . . . get the picture?
- Have you played your guitar through it? Never buy an amp without trying your guitar through it first to make sure it will do what you want it to do.
- Brand new or used? If used, then make sure the amp hasn't been so badly treated it has had the guts ripped out of it.
- When the amp is switched on listen. What for? Ideally, silence. Are there hums, buzzes, hisses? If so, beware.
- Check the speaker cone to make sure it's in one piece and not ripped or dented, or otherwise damaged.
- Test all the electrics, including switches and knobs, to make sure they work.
- Try out a variety of amps before you settle on the one you want to live with for a while.
- A tube amp will be heavier, but it will give you a warmer sound. A transistor amp will be easier to fix and will be more flexible if you want to use a variety of sounds with your guitar.

CHAPTER 10

How to
Record
Yourself

A Brief History

From about the turn of the twentieth century, the only way to capture sound was by first cutting a cylinder or a disk. Fairly quickly, the disk became the preferred method. In a recording studio, a wax disk was placed on a platter, and a needle attached to a microphone was placed at the outer edge of the disk. As the musician or group performed, the needle cut a continuous groove that recorded the sound.

When a vinyl impression of the master wax disk was made, to play the recording you essentially reversed the procedure. A needle was attached to a speaker, and when it was placed in the groove of the record and played at 78 revolutions per minute (rpm), you got a pretty accurate re-creation of the original recording session.

It was a bare bones, one-shot deal, however. No rerecording, no fixing "flubs," no using the disk again. Furthermore, it all had be done within three or four minutes, the length of time it took to go from the outside to the inside of the wax disk. Considering the demands of recording these disks, the performances that were captured are even more amazing when compared to what can be done today in the studio.

From the 1930s onward, tape recorders began to become available. These worked on the same principles as today: spools of tape coated with a magnetic oxide passed over a series of record and playback heads (or readers) on a tape machine. The big advantages of tape included the ability to edit the tape (using a razor blade and special glue or adhesive tape), the ability to rerecord or reuse the tape, and the ability to record longer pieces of music at one time. However, one drawback was that you couldn't make too many copies tape-to-tape because the quality of the recording would degenerate.

Multitrack recorders came into use in the 1940s, allowing for the recording of a rhythm track on one channel and for other tracks to be overdubbed on other channels. The subsequent recordings were then balanced, mixed, and "mastered" on a separate tape recorder. Up until the 1950s, everything had been *monoaural* or *mono*, the musical equivalent of black and white. Everything could be heard through one speaker. However, with the introduction of stereo, it was as though sound took on the musical equivalent of Technicolor. The invention of speakers with their own amplifiers meant that it was possible for each speaker to contain elements of the whole recording, creating the illusion that the drums were in the right speaker, the double bass in the left speaker, and the solo instrumentalist in the middle of the room in between the two speakers.

The psychedelic 1960s developed the stereo concept in wild and wooly ways as multitrack recorders went from four tracks to sixteen. By the 1970s this number had increased to twenty-four individual tracks.

In fact, during the 1970s, the development of quadraphonic sound meant that the listener could be placed in the middle of a room surrounded by four speakers. Somehow, it never caught on as it should, although it forms the basis of what is now known as "surround sound" for home entertainment systems.

The most radical of the digital inventions of the late 1980s and beyond was the invention of a computer protocol known as MIDI, which stands for Musical Instrument Digital Interface. This system of coding allows computers, synthesizers, drum machines, and digital effects units to talk to each other. It has revolutionized home recording, allowing garage musicians the ability to quickly and inexpensively produce professional-quality recordings. Paradoxically, the development of music genres that use digital sampling, such as hip-hop, means that you can be proficient in manipulating MIDI machines to create music without necessarily being proficient as a musician to create sounds.

The 1990s saw the greatest revolution in recording since the introduction of the tape recorder—digital technology. Digital audio tape (DAT) recorders replaced larger analog reel-to-reel machines, and the quality of recording became much cleaner. Background tape hiss was eliminated, and the final recording could be copied as many times as needed without the signal being degraded each time.

You can now buy software for the Macintosh and the PC that allows you to manipulate high-quality multitrack digital recordings that can be edited on-screen at the soundwave level. With the introduction of rewritable CDs and DVDs, and the increasing popularity of Sony Minidisk recorders and MP3 recorders, we are entering a brave new world of audio manipulation. It's perhaps worth reminding ourselves that the best recordings are about how the performer conveys emotion to the audience, and that the pallet of emotions we should draw upon is often much broader than many young musicians currently explore.

A word of warning: Recording is a vast and complicated field. This chapter can only introduce you to some of the concepts, and offer a few words of advice.

Engineers, Tape Ops, and Producers

In a small studio, many jobs are done by the engineer and/or the producer. However, in a larger studio, the engineer is responsible for recording all the performers and getting the final version down on tape, CD, or DVD. The average engineer knows which microphone is best for which instrument and which singer, and also has an intimate knowledge of the different kinds of recording equipment used to capture and manipulate the sound of the session. Many modern engineers are *tonemeisters*—engineers who got a university degree in recording engineering.

Tape ops are often trainee engineers. They basically serve as the studio gofers, doing everything the engineer and musicians don't want to do. Some of the world's best-known engineers and producers started off life as tape ops.

Producers are a wide array of people. Their principle role is to be an objective pair of ears for the performer, helping him or her achieve the sound they want. One example of a great producer is George Martin, a classically trained musician who, among many others, produced the Beatles by understanding and translating the ideas of Lennon and McCartney. Some have called him "the Fifth Beatle." Another is the brilliant jazz trumpeter and arranger Quincy Jones.

There are those who call themselves producers whose main expertise is *sampling*. They take a vocal track and build up layers of sound around the vocal, as in hip-hop recordings.

Do you need a producer for your recording? Only in the sense that you need someone who can objectively keep you on track and help you achieve your vision of what you want to create. Of course, this presumes you have a vision before you go into the studio. If you don't, the recording experience may end up being long, exhausting, and expensive—and the end result probably not very good.

Recording Studio Basics

Studio performing is very different from live gigs. The studio can be a cold and impersonal place, and the studio experience can be detrimental to the creative experience.

You have several options when it comes to recording:

- You can try to capture a live gig.
- You can go into a professional studio.
- You can try to create a professional demo using home equipment.

A professional studio will have pretty much all the hardware and software you'll need for your recording, but it will also cost you money. A twenty-four-track recording involving lots of overdubs and edits can be both time consuming and expensive.

Depending on your budget, you may want to consider a direct live recording, with no overdubs. This may take as much as a couple of hours to set up for sound, and then an hour per track to record. Alternatively, you may want to select a more adventurous multitrack recording. Here, the rhythm section (drums, bass, rhythm guitar, and/or piano) are recorded playing together. The lead guitar and vocal tracks are then overlayed afterwards. In general, the more tracks you overdub, the longer it takes to record and mix each track. It's possible you can spend all day (or longer) recording just one track this way, so be prepared. Either way, you will have to choose between the number of tracks you want to lay down, and what you can afford to pay for.

ALERT

Be sure to shop around before making a final decision on a recording studio. Don't allow your excitement to cloud your judgment.

Recording Studio Tips

- If you decide to use a studio, ask around and try to find musicians who have recorded there. See if they recommend the studio and find out why. Try not to rely on just one person's opinion, however. When you visit the studio, ask to hear samples of what they've done, and check out the condition of the equipment. Worn or poor equipment may mess with your recording and add to your time in the studio— and you will be paying for the studio on an hourly basis.
- Make sure the recording engineer and the producer are familiar and comfortable with the kind of music you want to record.
- Make sure you know exactly what you are going to get for your money. For example, does the studio fee include the final mix? Copies of the final mix? Studio-owned instruments you can use? What are the other expenses?
- Unless money is no object, record material that you have rehearsed and know well. A studio is a daunting place, and not conducive to jamming, unless you're experienced.
- Make sure your equipment (strings, cords, amp, and so forth) is in good condition before you bring it into the studio.
- Be on time, particularly if it's not your gig and someone else is paying for the studio time.
- Rather than trying for ten hastily recorded tracks, opt for four or five well-recorded ones.
- Make use of what's at hand, particularly other musicians. Lay down all the rhythm tracks, for example, and then come back if necessary to overdub the lead and vocal tracks.
- Keep the session a "closed set," and don't make it a party. Have fun, but don't be distracted by having friends and acquaintances hanging out, getting in the way, and trying to act as "co-producer."
- If you're unhappy with something, rerecord it. Don't be easily satisfied with the old saw, "We can fix it in the mix." Trust us, you'll hear that clunking note until the day you die if you don't! Don't be too much of a perfectionist, however. You have to strike a balance here.
- Make sure you have some kind of final mix policy before you start the session. All the musicians involved will be focused on their

performance alone, and someone is going to have to call the shots for the final mix down. If it's your record it shouldn't be a problem. If you're a sidesman (or woman), you may have to deal with—and accept—someone else's opinion on what the overall sound will be like, and your place in it.

• Do the final mix a week or more after the initial recording, so that you can come back to the session with fresher ears.

Jack Wilkins's Ten Commandments for the Studio

1. *If it ain't broke, don't fix it.* Whether you record on your Fostex at home or forty-eight-track digital in a world-class studio, remember Duke Ellington's maxim: If It Sounds Good, It Is Good. If you like the sound you're getting (a) don't change it, and (b) if you have to change it, remember what made it sound good in the first place.

2. *If it's broke, fix it.* The corollary to Number 1 is that if it sounds lousy on tape, you won't be able to "fix it in the mix." If a track is not cutting it, change it or kill it. Try equalizing, compressing, and editing (if it doesn't take too much time at the end of the session), or adding another microphone. The key is to be honest with yourself. If necessary, admit that (a) your favorite overdub isn't working; (b) the musical idea isn't cutting it; (c) the vocalist or instrumentalist is "off" today; or (d) the performer just can't cut it. One way or another, move on.

3. *Keep it simple.* Mixing is like cooking: Too many spices can ruin the dish. Move faders sparingly, 1 dB at a time. The mix always sounds great at 10 on the big speakers. The trick is to make it sound great at 3 on little speakers.

4. *Happy people make good music.* If something personal is bugging you, leave it at home. If something in the studio bugs you, try not to ruin a good mood. It can stop a session dead. Good music comes when everyone—musicians and technicians alike—are having fun.

5. *Be prepared.* Be rehearsed and bring everything you need. Losing an hour of studio time because you don't have a $5 set of strings or a

9-volt battery is infuriating, costly, and drives everyone in the studio crazy. Be early! The clock starts at the appointed hour, not when you get there, and there's never enough time.

6. *Speaking of time. . .* If you have tempo troubles, rehearse the track slower. If anything sounds out of tune, check it. Use an empty track to record and try to mix great performances with minor time or intonation problems. If you were inspired, you may never quite get that feeling again.

7. *Respect studio staff.* Try not to be a pain for the studio staff, but remember, if you're paying, they're working for you. If the engineer says that something sounds great and you disagree, don't let it slide. Just pick your battles. If the vocal sounds awful, insist that it's done the way you want it. If that cute little overdub stinks, mute it in the mix.

8. *Know what to record.* No amount of technical magic can compensate for mediocrity. When you gig, the audience tells you what they like. Nine times out of ten, the songs that come alive are the ones the public like best. Determine your list of tunes in advance based on the feedback you've received.

9. *Beat the pre-demo blues.* Don't put endless hours into a home demo and then go into a real studio to try to re-create it. Instead, try to channel your energy into the studio recording session.

10. *Know when to go home.* When your fingers get sore and your ears get tired, even if you have more time booked, go home and come back another day when you're fresher. Slow time in the studio comes in the beginning, as you are trying to get the right sound. Wasted time comes at the end. Remember what is important: (a) rhythm tracks; (b) vocals; (c) solos; (d) overdubs; and (e) effects.

Creating a Home Studio

When you're planning to create a home setup, you need to consider how much money and space you can devote to the studio. A dedicated garage space or basement with a permanent studio setup will give you a much different sound and setup to a few mikes, a Fostex DAT recorder, and a MIDI-ready Macintosh computer in your front room.

The science of acoustics is too involved to get into here, but an empty room may sound very "live" (clap your hands in such a room and listen to the echo); the same room with curtains, carpeting, and furniture will sound much "deader." Consider what you are going to record and how best to record it. Drums, for example, may need to be in a deader space than vocals, which may need a more live environment.

ALERT

Before jumping into the commitment of a home studio, carefully consider the cost and time involved. To get the best results, you need to be dedicated to the outcome of the project.

Are you going to use an analog, old-fashioned, four-track reel-to-reel recorder such as Teac's Portastudio or the Fostex "X" series of cassette tape recorders, or a more modern digital system? Most people go for the digital system these days, but money will dictate what you can afford. Perhaps you'll be able to pick up some decent secondhand equipment on eBay, or a local store.

Digital systems come in two basic flavors:

1. Real-time tape machines
2. Computer-based, hard-disk recording systems.

Real-Time Recorders

One of the most popular systems is the ADAT system, developed by Alesis and also used by Fostex. Eight tracks can be recorded individually or together on super VHS videotape. Through the magic of MIDI, digital recording allows a series of machines to be linked together as "slave" machines that can be controlled by a "master" machine if needed.

Hard-Disk Systems

The most common hard-disk systems are computer-based. For years the Apple Macintosh reigned supreme, but these days there are similar systems for a PC. One advantage of a hard-disk system is that the recording can be easily edited at an almost "atomic" note-by-note level. Another is that you can cut and paste whole sections as easily as if you were using a word processor. Recordings can also be sequencer-based, which means digital sounds can be mixed with MIDI tracks.

Home Recording Systems

Apple Macintosh

A lot of recording studios use Macintosh computers for their DAT installations. If you decide to use a Mac, you'll need the following:

- A PCI-bus Power Mac, especially if the computer has PCI expansion slots and 16-bit audio capabilities. If you buy a used machine, try to find a machine that can be upgraded to a G3 or G4 processor. Get as much RAM installed as you can afford. The absolute minimum you should have is 64MB, although 128MB or more will make things run much more smoothly. The iMac, Mac OS X (OS "Ten"), and G4 are the newest Mac computers. They come standard with an IDE hard drive and CD-ROM drive, and decent quality 16-bit audio built in, and USB and FireWire (IEEE1394) ports, which means you'll have to buy brand-new USB MIDI interfaces, or get a USB-to-serial adapter and install USB and MIDI driver updates.
- A big SCSI or FireWire hard drive (at least 40GB or more is best). The FireWire interface is probably the interface of the future. It can be used for hard drives and should be usable with CD-recordable drives, too. FireWire allows for hot-swappable connection of up to 64 devices, and allows for a theoretical maximum throughput of around 40MB/second. There is no such thing as a "Macintosh-only" SCSI or FireWire hard drive. SCSI is SCSI and FireWire is FireWire, whether in a Mac or a PC, which does simplify matters somewhat.

Software is generally more expensive on the Macintosh platform, but some of it is pretty good, such as Mark of the Unicorn Digital Performer, TC/Works Spark XL, and Bias Peak. There is also some Mac music shareware around, though nothing like what is available for a PC.

Windows-Based PCs

Once upon a time, the Windows-based PC platform was no match for Macintosh in the artistic arenas of sight and sound. That is no longer true. If you're willing to become a bit of a computer nerd, you can get a lot of power for less money than buying a Mac.

Hardware

Pentium III or better, AMD, or Celeron chip processors are the most widely compatible with all the various soundcards and other peripherals for use with PCs. Using anything slower than a Pentium 166 will make it very hard to work on stereo digital audio files for CD mastering. Stick to well-known name brands and you should be okay. However, pay attention to compatibility issues between peripherals. If you're really set on a particular soundcard or audio interface, check on the manufacturer's Web site for links to user forums or newsgroups where you can read about users' experiences with various types of peripherals and software. You may find that advanced features of a particular soundcard won't work in your favorite audio program, or that a certain video card will cause problems in your particular system.

For the operating system, most people will run either Microsoft Windows 98 SE, Windows ME, Windows 2000, or Windows NT 4.0. If you intend to use USB or FireWire devices, you'll be better off using Windows 98 or Windows 2000.

If you are doing extensive MIDI work, you'll need good MIDI timing and lots of MIDI channels. By turning off the extra bells and whistles that Windows 98 installs by default (check out the Tweak UI program on the installation disk under tools/reskit/powertools), you can usually get very good MIDI timing in your sequencer applications. Also, check out 98 Lite (*www.98lite.com*) for tips on how to strip Windows 98 down to its bare essentials.

A word of caution: Software that requires Microsoft DirectX 5.0 or later will probably not work under Windows NT. This includes software synths like GigaSampler, Seer Systems Reality, FruityLoops, or Roland Virtual Sound Canvas. There is an unofficial, unsupported patch that installs DirectX 5.0 in NT, but there are absolutely no guarantees with these kinds of "hacks." Search on the Internet for a file named NT4DX5.zip, but use your own judgment.

Linux is fast becoming a viable OS alternative, and there is a lot of work going on aimed at making Linux a workable OS for the masses. A few soundcards are currently supported in Linux, including the Sonorus STUDI/O, SEK'D Prodif Gold, Zefiro Acoustics ZA-2, Aureal Vortex 2 (Turtle Beach Montego II and Diamond MX-300), and the Ensoniq AudioPCI (audio only), while the venerable Roland MPU-401 is supported for MIDI I/O.

Anyone interested in exploring Linux should check out *www.4front-tech.com* and *http://sound.condorow.net,* the Linux MIDI and Sound Application Web site.

PCs don't always come with built-in sound, so you may have to buy and install your own soundcard. It pays to do your homework before you buy a card. You will want either a big IDE or SCSI hard drive (at least 40GB or more). A SCSI drive will give you better performance.

Software

There is a lot of high-quality Windows music "shareware" available on the Internet. Don't be afraid to try these programs out; some are excellent. Two great shareware stereo sound editors are Cool Edit 2000 and GoldWave. Of course, there are tremendous commercial Windows sound editors, such as Sound Forge, Cool Edit Pro, Samplitude, Steinberg WaveLab, and SAW, as well as MIDI/Audio sequencers such as Cakewalk Pro Audio, Steinberg Cubase VST, and Emagic Logic Audio on the high end, with PG Music Power Tracks Pro Audio and FASoft-n-Track.

ALERT

Can't decide which system to use? Remember that the more complex the system you choose, the more time you will have to spend learning how to use and manipulate the result, and the less time you will spend playing music.

There are a number of things that can mess up a PCs ability to play and record clean-sounding digital audio—resource-greedy device drivers, overly intrusive antivirus programs, and fancy fax software come to mind immediately. If your first priority is *music,* make sure you fine-tune your system for that, rather than, say, playing games.

CHAPTER 11

How to
Practice

Good Habits

The key to good practice habits is consistency. Ten minutes a day—every day—is better than eight hours once a week on a Saturday afternoon. Your fingers have to learn a "muscle memory" of how to form the chords and where to go and what to do, and you have to get over the slight soreness of your fingertips until the calluses build up. (A hint: If your fingertips get sore, take a break and dip them in some rubbing alcohol.)

FACTS

Knowing how to practice, and what to practice, can mean the difference between spending hours spinning your wheels in one place, and advancing by leaps and bounds with only an hour or two a day.

First Things First

The first thing you should try to get is a professional teacher, a decent instrument, and a good method book. (You can find a list of some useful books in the Appendix.)

You have to be honest with yourself about how much time you can put into practicing. Ideally, your practice time and place should be the same every day. You should practice in a well-lit area with a comfortable chair and a music stand.

Write out a schedule for yourself and stick to it. It is absolutely imperative that you practice in a relaxed manner. If you strain, you'll run the risk of muscle problems with your shoulders or your hands. Take lots of breaks during your practice session, partly to relax and help the muscles, and partly to ensure that you don't build in mistakes into your playing technique in an attempt to "get to the next stage" as quickly as possible.

If your hands start to tighten or cramp, stop and take deep breaths, which will ease the tension and calm you down at the same time.

Take walks. Remember that—paradoxically—you will improve much faster if you allow your hands and fingers to develop slowly and at their own speed.

A Practice Schedule

It would be great if you could practice two hours every day, but few of us can. Practicing is a highly personal thing and what works for one person doesn't always work for someone else. That said, there *are* certain things you should try to do.

Be consistent. Try to spend five or ten minutes every day on the same thing. Repetition breeds a familiarity which creates a confidence that will help you on to the next stage. This can become tedious and boring, however, so you have to strike a balance between maintaining your interest and perfecting your skills.

If you can't do something every day, try to do it two or three times a week. Again, the keys are repetition and consistency.

Spread the work over several days. Be sure you do this every week consistently.

For example:

Monday: Do some method book exercises and major scales.

Tuesday: Do some picking and strumming exercises, open string chords, and minor scales.

Wednesday: Work on more method book items and music-reading skills.

Thursday: Learn some harmony and work on more songs.

Friday: Start the sequence all over again.

Remember, take lots of breaks and stay relaxed. If something is hard, try it a couple of times and then go on to something else. In a while, return to the hard exercise and chip away at it drop by drop.

Beginning Player's Practice Schedule (two hours)

20 minutes: work through four pages of method book

20 minutes: practice major scales (open position)

20 minutes: spend time learning major, minor, and 7th open string chords

20 minutes: alternate right-hand picking exercises

20 minutes: study music theory and harmony

10 minutes: practice a few barre (see page 206) chords

10 minutes: strum chords to some simple songs per the method book

You should try to stick to this for seven to ten days, although there is no real time limit; everyone learns at a different rate. When you're comfortable, you can change it around a little.

These principles of practice are really the same whatever level of playing you've reached. The only difference is the kinds of thing you'll be practicing.

Intermediate Player's Practice Schedule (two hours)

20 minutes: work through six to eight pages of intermediate method book

20 minutes: practice major and minor scales (up to 5th position)

20 minutes: practice chords

20 minutes: work on right-hand alternate consecutive picking exercises

20 minutes: learn to read music in different positions

10 minutes: work on triad and 7th chord arpeggios

10 minutes: learn chords and melodies to more advanced songs, such as "Blackbird," "Over the Rainbow," "Satin Doll," etc.

The intermediate schedule may look daunting now, but by the time you reach that level, it will make pretty good sense to you.

LESSON 1

Holding the Guitar and Writing Music

Sitting

Before you start playing, you need to be able to comfortably cradle the guitar so that you're relaxed when you play. There are a number of way of doing this. Let's begin with sitting.

The traditional, classical guitar position is to raise the neck of the guitar to about 45 degrees from the vertical—that is, you want the head of the instrument about level with your shoulder, while the "waist" of the guitar rests on your left thigh. Place your left foot on an adjustable footstool to help create this effect. By holding the neck at this angle, you get the maximum positioning of your left hand on the fretboard, and your right hand over the strings. The hands do not support the neck in this position.

FIGURE 1-1:
Classical pose

FIGURE 1-2:
Informal
sitting pose

The more informal seated position is to rest the waist of the guitar on your right thigh, while the inside of your right arm holds the body of the instrument in place, and your left hand gives slight support to the neck.

If you have a solid-bodied electric guitar, the seated position can be awkward because the weight of the head and neck will dip down, making the guitar hard to play. You'll need to use a shoulder strap.

Standing

If you decide to play standing up, make sure you buy a good strap that will comfortably support the weight of the guitar and not cut into your shoulder at the same time.

FIGURE 1-3:
Standing
pose

The guitar should hang comfortably against your body, leaving both your arms free. If the strap is adjusted properly, the neck of the guitar should be at about a 45-degree angle. The bridge should be about level with your waist, and the head about level with your shoulder.

We know, you saw some rock idol playing with the guitar at his ankle level, and it looked really cool. After you know what you're doing, you can adjust the instrument any way you want. But for now, as a beginner, don't make life harder for yourself than it has to be. Playing with the guitar slung too low can really strain your hands and wrists.

Left-Hand Position

To begin with, the best way to fret a note cleanly is to exert the maximum pressure using your fingertips. The key is to develop a good left-hand technique. First, let the edge of the neck of the guitar rest in the palm of your left hand. You'll notice that your thumb and fingers automatically fall to either side of the neck. Now place the left-hand thumb in the middle of the back of the neck so that there is a nice space between the neck and your palm. You should be able to pivot your whole hand on the ball of your thumb without banging into the neck.

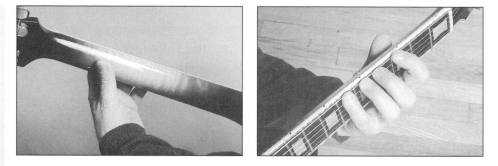

FIGURE 1-4:
Placing the
thumb in the
middle of the
back of the neck.

FIGURE 1-5:
Holding the string
against the fret
with the fingertip
pad (Notice: Each
finger to a fret.)

When you fret a note, use the tip or pad of your finger to press the note firmly to the fingerboard. If you put your thumb immediately behind the place where you're pressing the string to the fretboard (as if you're trying to pinch thumb and finger together through the neck), you'll get maximum pressure on the note and it will sound clean.

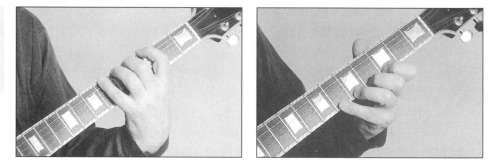

FIGURE 1-6:
Left-hand
position

FIGURE 1-7

In classical guitar parlance, they talk about the right and left hands looking like two swans' necks. That may be a bit much for most players, but try the following exercise. Place the tip of your first finger on the first string at the first fret. (Look at **FIGURE 1-8**.) Now pluck the string with your right-hand thumb by the sound hole.

In **FIGURE 1-9**, each vertical line represents a string. Each horizontal line represents a fretwire. The double line at the top represents the guitar nut. The black dot or number represents the finger you should use to stop that string at that fret—in this case, at the note F on the first string.

Press the string to the fretboard roughly in the middle of the fret (between the fretwires). If you press too close to a fretwire, the string may be muted; too far away and the string may buzz. To make sure you don't mute other strings, make a point of using your fingertips and keeping your fingers as vertical as possible to the strings by arching your wrist slightly (like a swan's neck). The classical guitar technique helps in this regard.

A lot of players let their left-hand thumb come over the top of the neck. They even use it to fret bass notes. This is perfectly fine, but it's hard for beginners to do. Remember, the more your hand is cramped up, the harder it is to play the note well (that is, without any buzzing sound), and the more your muscles may ache.

FIGURE 1-8
FIGURE 1-9

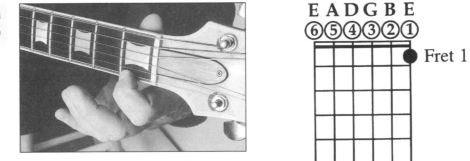

As soon as your hand or fingers get sore or start to hurt, stop! It will take a little time for the strength in your fingers to build up. Playing a little bit often is better than playing a lot in one go.

Right-Hand Position

The right hand can be used fingerstyle, which means that each finger of the right hand manipulates the strings (as in classical or folk/blues fingerpicking styles). Alternately, you can hold a plectrum or pick in your right hand to strum various rhythms or pick out notes on the strings.

Fingerstyle

The basic fingerstyle position is to use the fingernails to pluck the strings. (Initially, you may use your fingertips as well.) The fingers are held vertical to the strings with a slight arch in the wrist. (Remember the idea of a swan's neck?) The thumb plays the three bass strings, while the first finger plucks the third string, the second finger the second string, and the third finger the first string. (The little finger is not usually used.)

FIGURE 1-10:
Right-hand
position

For the moment, it's probably a good idea to practice strumming all six strings first with a pick, and then using just your thumb. The key is to place your fingertips on the fingerplate to anchor your hand, and then brush your thumb across all the strings. We'll discuss more complex fingerpicking and pick techniques further on.

Holding a Pick

The size and thickness of a plectrum (also known as a *pick*) can vary greatly. In the beginning, you'll want one that has a medium size and thickness. Buy yourself two or three and experiment.

Let the pick lie flat on your first finger, and then comfortably hold it in place with your thumb. You can then use it to strum the string with up-and-down motions. The movement comes from your wrist, not your fingers.

FIGURE 1-11:
Holding a pick

FIGURE 1-12:
Using the pick
to strum

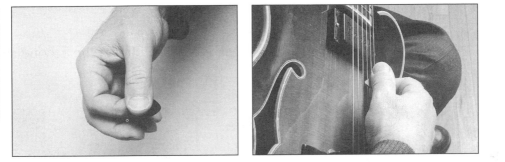

To get a feel of what to do, take your right hand and extend the fingers, thumb and first finger lightly touching at the tip. Now, with the fingertips still touching, shake your hand up and down at the wrist in a gentle, comfortable motion. This is the motion you want to use to strum the guitar strings.

Getting It Down on Paper

There are three basic ways to write down music for the guitar.

Chords and Slashes

The first way uses chord symbols and slashes, which represent the number of times you should strum a chord. Each slash represents one down stroke or strum of a chord.

FIGURE 1-13:
Written music
using chord
symbols and
slashes

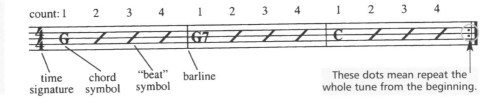

Chords are also written down in boxes, which are really representations of the fingerboard. Each vertical line is a string, and each horizontal line is a fretwire.

FIGURE 1-14:
E (Major)

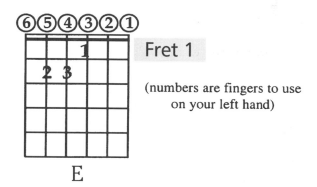

Fret 1

(numbers are fingers to use on your left hand)

E

Each circle or number represents a place where you should put your finger on the fretboard and the finger you should use to stop the note. The name of the chord is written under the diagram.

If you look at the chord diagram you'll see that the chord has a distinctive "shape." Let's call this one the "E" shape. Each finger has a certain place it should be on the fingerboard in order to play the E chord. If you move your fingers over a string (i.e., the chord shape starts not on the String 5 but on the String 4), then the "E" shape will make the chord "A minor." (Don't worry about why for now.) It's a good idea to think about chords as "shapes" that can be moved around the fingerboard. It will come in very useful later on when we explore the issue more.

The left-hand fingers are numbered as shown in **FIGURE 1-15**.

FIGURE 1-15:
The hand,
numbered

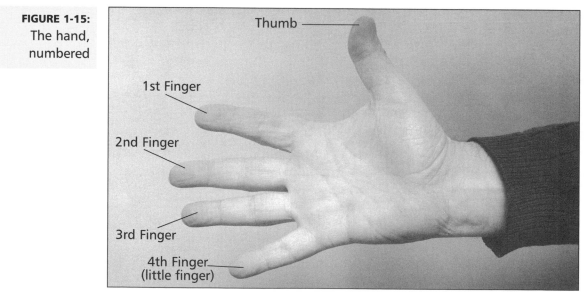

Guitar Tablature

Another way to write down music is using guitar tablature.

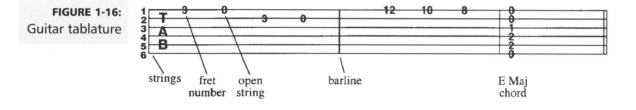

FIGURE 1-16:
Guitar tablature

Here, each line represents a string on the guitar, with the top line the first string, and the bottom line the sixth string. The numbers on each line represent the fret you need to stop in order to get a note. You can show complex fingerings this way, including chords and melodies.

Standard Notation

Finally, there is standard notation. This looks a lot like tablature, except instead of six lines there are only five.

FIGURE 1-17:
Standard
notation

We will get into how to read music later on. It's enough to know that you can do a lot more with written music than with almost any other system of musical notation, and learning to read isn't that hard. Music only has 7 letters—C, D, E, F, G, A, and B—and then it starts all over again. With a little regular practice, you'll be reading music in no time.

LESSON 2

First Songs
and Chords

Chords C and G7

Now you're going to learn to strum some songs. To do this, you'll need to learn a few chords. A chord is made when three or more strings are played together, usually by strumming down with a pick or plectrum, or by using your thumb.

The chords we are going to show you now are easy versions of fuller open string chords you'll learn later. Their names are C and G7. Try to memorize the names of the chords and the shapes they make.

C

G7

To play the chord C (major), put your first finger on the second string at the first fret. Press hard. Strum Strings 1, 2, and 3 together four times. You've now strummed four beats. When it is written this way, it is a bar of music: | C / / / |

Strum the chord four more times. You've now strummed two bars of C. (| C / / / | C / / / |)

To play the chord G7, put your first finger on the first string at the first fret. Play the first three strings again, strumming four times.

Play the C chord four more times. And then another four times. Play G7 four times. Now play C four times.

Surprise! You've successfully played the song "Merrily We Roll Along." This chord slash style is illustrated below. The 4/4 at the beginning means count and play four beats in every bar. If it was 3/4 at the beginning, what do you think it means? (The answer is that you would play and count three beats in the bar.) The bars are created by bar lines that look like this: " | " It is usual to write four bars per line and then go to another line. In "Merrily . . ." for example, the first bar is C for four beats, and the second bar is also C for four beats. The third bar is G7 for four beats, and the fourth bar is C for four beats. The next line is a repeat of the first line, so that the song has a total of eight bars altogether.

Merrily We Roll Along

4/4 C / / / | C / / / | G7 / / / | C / / / |
    C / / / | C / / / | G7 / / / | C / / / ||

Merrily we roll along, roll along, roll along,
Merrily we roll along, over the deep blue sea.

This is going to take some practice. You may find that your fingertips get sore. The strings will buzz if you stop them in the wrong part of the fret or don't press hard enough. As you change chords while you strum, it's a challenge to jump your finger smoothly from the first string to the second string and back again. But don't get disheartened. Remember, everyone who has ever played the guitar—from Segovia to Pat Metheny to Eric Clapton—has had to go through this stage, and they found it just as awkward and just as frustrating.

The trick is to practice slowly and try to aim for good technique. Slightly arch your wrist, use your fingertips, and press firmly with your thumb in the middle of the back of the neck as you press down with your fingertip to stop the string. Try to eliminate all sounds of buzzing. Keep your other fingers out of the way.

Try this tune:

Go Tell Aunt Rhodie

4/4 C / / / | C / / / | G7 / / / | C / / / |
     C / / / | C / / / | G7 / / / | C / / / ||
Go tell Aunt Rhodie, go tell Aunt Rhodie,
Go tell Aunt Rhodie, the old gray goose is dead.

Chords D7 and G

Now let's try some more chords. The first chord is D7. This chord is going to use three fingers. Study the chord chart. Remember, each number represents a finger. (Third finger on second fret of first string; first finger on first fret of second string; second finger on second fret of third string.)

FIGURE 2-2(a):
D7

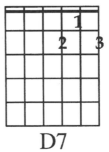

D7

FIGURE 2-2(b):
G

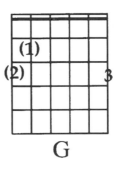

G

This chord is going to take some practice before it sounds clear. Work at it. A good exercise is to try to press hard and play the chord. Then relax your hand but keep the shape of the chord made by the fingers, raise them off the guitar strings, and then put the shape back on the strings—again, pressing hard. This may help build "muscle memory," so that the fingers "remember" where they should go to form this chord.

The next chord is the full open-string version of the chord of G. If you have trouble with this, just play the note on the first string and strum the first four open strings.

Twinkle, Twinkle Little Star

4/4 G / / / | C / G / | C / G / | D7 / G / |
      G / C / | G / D7 / | G / C / | G / D7 / |
      G / / / | C / G / | C / G / | D7 / G / ||

Twinkle, twinkle little star, how I wonder where you are
Up above the world so high, like a diamond in the sky,
Twinkle, twinkle little star, how I wonder where you are.

Notice that in this song, in the second and third bars and elsewhere, you'll play two beats of C and then two beats of G. This is a hard tune to play, so practice it a lot. The whole idea is for you to get comfortable changing chords.

Amazing Grace

Note: This tune has a "key signature" of 3/4. This means you strum three beats to the bar. Notice also that the second bar is blank. This means that you should repeat the previous bar. So bar two would be another three beats of G, as would be bar six. Bar eight will be three beats of D7, etc.

3/4 G / / | | C / / | G / / |
      G / / | | D7 / / | |
      G / / | | C / / | G / / |
      G / / | D7 / / | G / / | ||

Try these fuller versions of the chords C and G7, and then go back and practice the songs using the full versions.

FIGURE 2-3(a):
C

FIGURE 2-3(b):
G7

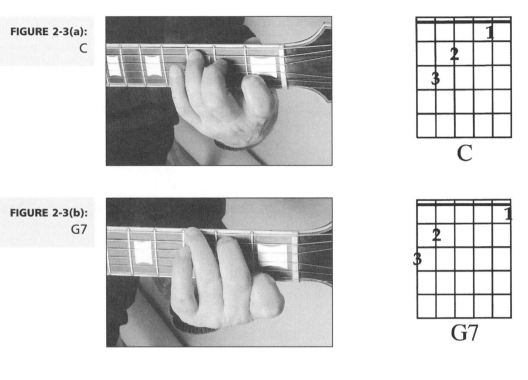

She'll Be Coming Round the Mountain

```
4/4  G / / / |            |           |              |
     G / / / |            | D / / / | |              |
     G / / / |            | C / / / | |              |
     G / / / | D / / / | G / / / |              ||
```

The following are the full versions of some of the songs noted in this chapter. Use the tablature if necessary.

FIGURE 2-4:
Merrily

Merrily

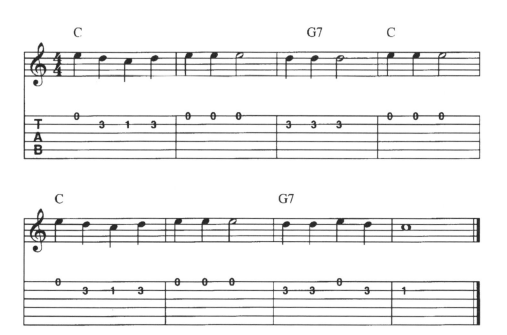

Use the tabulature to "read" these notes and play them if you can't read music yet.

FIGURE 2-5:
Aunt Rhodie

Aunt Rhodie

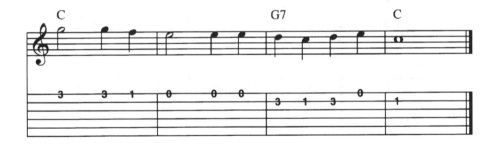

FIGURE 2-6:
Twinkle, Twinkle
Little Star

Twinkle, Twinkle Little Star

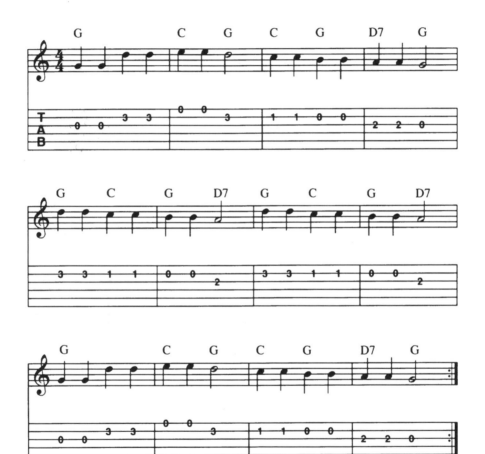

FIGURE 2-7:
Amazing Grace

Amazing Grace

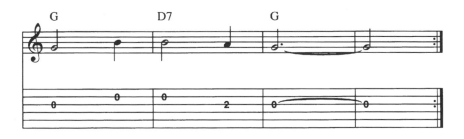

FIGURE 2-8:
Coming Round
the Mountain

Coming Round the Mountain *

count: 1 2 3 4

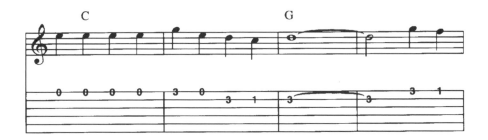

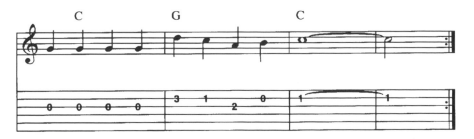

*Note: This is in a different key than in the text. See chord families in Lesson 3.

LESSON 3

Picking and More Open-String Chords

Right-Hand Picking

While you're still working on the chords you've already learned, let's look at some right-hand things you can study.

By now, you can see that holding and using a pick is a bit more complicated than just brushing the strings with your thumb. If you haven't done it already, play the songs in Lesson 2 using your thumb the first time through, and then the pick the next time through.

There are two distinct ways of hitting the string with a pick: a *downstroke* and an *upstroke*. To make a downstroke, use the tip of the pick and push down. The symbol is ⊓ .

Upstrokes are the reverse. The tip of the pick is used to pull up on the string. The symbol is V .

If you want to master using a pick, you need to become very comfortable mixing downstrokes and upstrokes. Otherwise, you will never get any kind of speed and articulation in your playing.

FIGURE 3-1 includes some exercises to help develop right-hand picking. They use open strings and are written in both music notation and tablature. Things are a lot more complicated if you're left handed because you'll need a left-handed guitar. If you get one, then just do everything in a mirror image, substituting left hand for right hand and vice versa.

FIGURE 3-1:
Right-hand
picking exercises

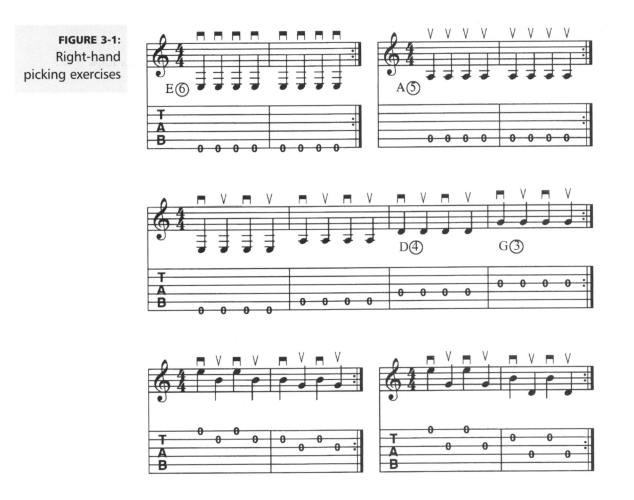

One of the great things about this exercise is that you also learn to read music at the same time. (See, we told you it wouldn't be difficult.)

Minor Chord

Let's try a new chord. It's called a *minor chord* (written with a small *mi),* and it has a sad or bluesy quality to it. We'll show you three minor chords: Ami, Emi, and Dmi.

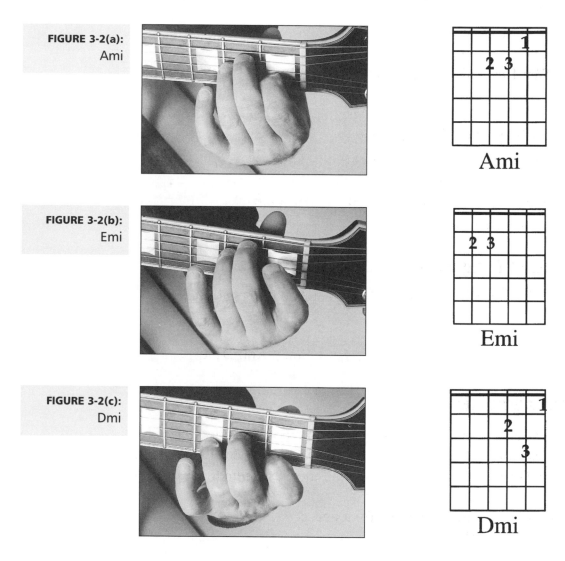

FIGURE 3-2(a): Ami

Ami

FIGURE 3-2(b): Emi

Emi

FIGURE 3-2(c): Dmi

Dmi

Drunken Sailor

4/4   Dmi / / / | | C / / / | |
       Dmi / / / | | C / / / | Dmi / / / ||

What shall we do with the drunken sailor?
What shall we do with the drunken sailor?
What shall we do with the drunken sailor?
Earl-eye in the morning

Wey, Hey and up she rises,
Wey, Hey and up she rises,
Wey, Hey and up she rises,
Earl-eye in the morning

Swing Low, Sweet Chariot

4/4 (Swing) || D / / / | G / D / | G / D / | Emi / A / |
                D / / / | G / D / | D / A / | D / / / ||

Note: The first word of the song is in parentheses at the beginning so you know where you are starting.

Auld Lang Syne

4/4 (Should) || G / / / | D / / / | G / / / | C / / / |
               G / / / | D / / / | Emi / Ami D| G / / / ||
               G / / / | D / / / | G / / / | C / / / |
               G / / / | D / / / | Emi / Ami D| G / / / ||

Chord Families

Chords go together in families (or, as it is more formally called, *keys*). For example, a G7 chord is part of the C family, and a D7 chord is part of the G family. Play those chords and they just seem to fit naturally together. A D7 chord, for example, does not lead to a C chord nearly as well as it leads to a G chord. Try it and see.

Chords break down into three basic types:

Major chords (like G or C), which sound happy.

Minor chords (like Ami and Dmi), which sound sad.

Dominant seventh chords (like G7 or D7), which sound slightly jazzy and seem to want to lead us to resolve to a major chord.

Okay, now let's show you three more chords. These are part of the key (family) of A: A, D, and E7.

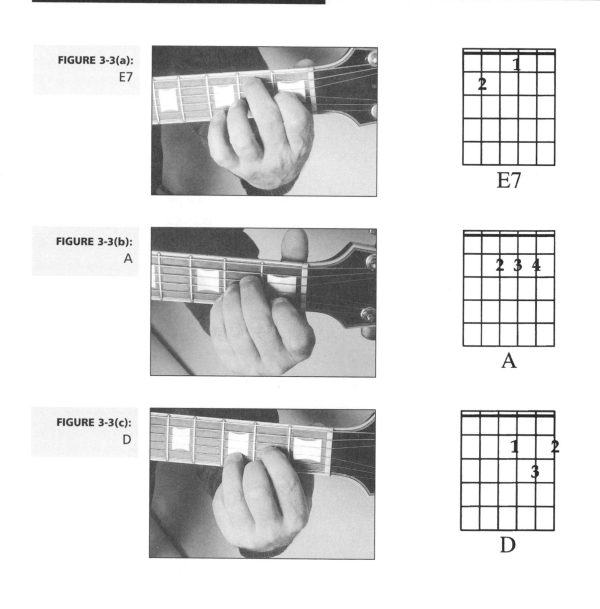

FIGURE 3-3(a):
E7

E7

FIGURE 3-3(b):
A

A

FIGURE 3-3(c):
D

D

Yankee Doodle

4 / 4 D / / / / | D / A / | D / / / | D / A / |
D / / / | G / / / | A / / / | D / / / ||

Kumbaya

4/4 (Kum-ba-) || A / / / | / / D / | A / / / | |
                   A / / / | / / D / | E7 / / / | |
                   A / / / | / / D / | A / / / | / / D / |
                   A / / / | / / E7 / | A / / / | ||

When Johnny Comes Marching Home

3/4 (When) || Ami / / | | | |
            Emi / / | | | |
            Ami / / | | | |
            C   / / | | | |
            Ami / / | | Dmi / / | |
            Ami / / | | E7 / / | |
            Ami / / | E7 / / / | Ami / / | E7 / / / |
            Ami / / | | | ||

In **FIGURES 3-4(a), (b),** and **(c),** are all the open-string chords you should learn. One of the things that makes learning chords easier is that families (keys) share the same chords, or variations on them. So once you know how to play a C chord, or an E7 chord, it will be the same regardless of the sequence you find it in.

Buy some song books, or look on the Web for some song sheets you can download. Make sure they have the chords to the tunes printed on them so you can practice the songs.

Spend some time working on changing smoothly from one chord to another as you strum. Some of these chords involve using your first finger to stop more than one string. To do this, use the fatty part of your finger. Initially, you may want to lay your second finger on top of your first finger to help you make just enough contact with the strings on the fretboard so they don't buzz.

If you pay attention, you'll notice some chords in the same key are missing. That's because they can't be played with open strings. You will soon learn how to play these chords.

FIGURE 3-4(a):
Open-string
chords

Key (family) of G

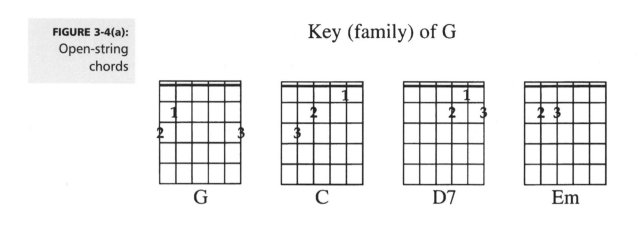

G   C   D7   Em

Key of A

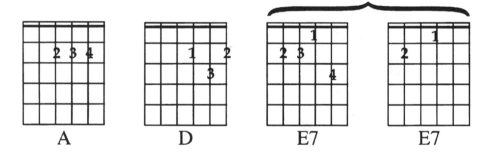

A   D   E7   E7

(alternate fingering)

Key of C

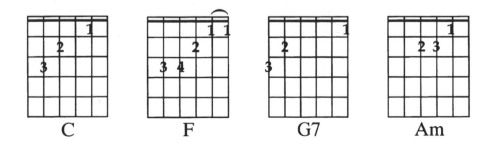

C   F   G7   Am

FIGURE 3-4(b):
Open-string
chords

Key of D

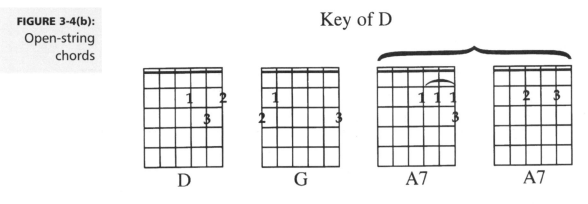

D   G   A7   A7

(alternate fingering)

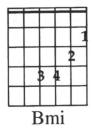

Bmi

Key of E

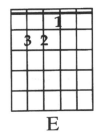

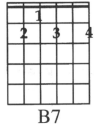

E   A   B7

FIGURE 3-4(c):
Open-string
chords

Key of F

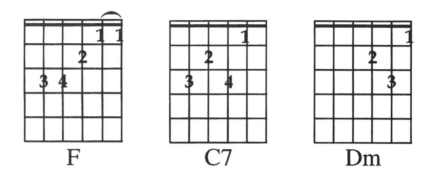

F   C7   Dm

Notice in **FIGURE 3-5(a)** that each finger of the left hand should play a particular fret. The first finger plays the first fret, second finger plays the second fret, third finger plays the third fret, and the fourth or little finger plays the fourth fret.

Below is a left-hand fingering exercise. Notice that you should play this using each finger to a fret as we've discussed. (Normally, you would not play the "B" on the fourth fret third string, and also the open second string. But for the purposes of this exercise go ahead and do it anyway.)

FIGURE 3-5(a):
Left-hand
finger exercises

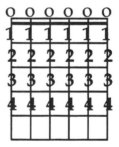

FIGURE 3-5(b):
Each finger
to a fret

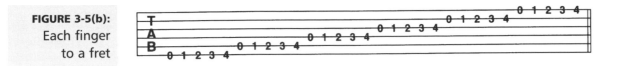

1st finger = 1st fret
2nd finger = 2nd fret, and so on
Practice alternate picking as well.

Here's some sheet music for some more songs that you probably recognize, which you can practice using what you've learned so far.

Enjoy.

FIGURE 3-6:
Jingle Bells

Jingle Bells

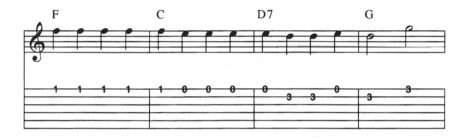

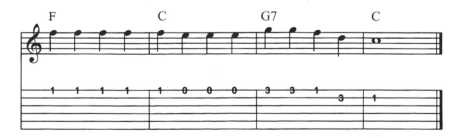

FIGURE 3-7:
Simple Blues
in E

Simple Blues in E

FIGURE 3-8:
Simple Minor
Blues

Simple Minor Blues

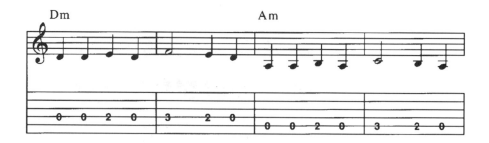

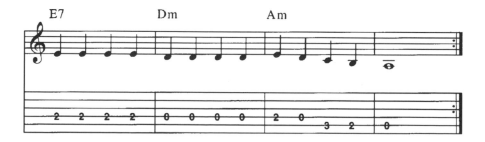

LESSON 4

The Basics of Reading Music

Rhythm and Time

Having a good knowledge of "where the beat is" and playing in time are paramount for a musician. As Duke Ellington once wrote, "It don't mean a thing, if it ain't got that swing . . ."

Time breaks down into two elements: *rhythm*, or the "feel" of a piece of music; and *tempo*, or the speed you play at. Music often has a suggested tempo marking on it that may look like this: ♩ = 120. The number 120 refers to the number of beats per minute (bpm) on a metronome. It denotes how fast (or slow) the piece should be played. The lower the number, the slower the piece of music. The higher the number, the faster the piece of music. In general, these are the accepted tempos (tempi, to be more precise), each of which has an Italian descriptive term.

Grave: very slow, slower than 40 bpm

Lento: slow, 40 to 60 bpm

Adagio: slow (at ease), 60 to 75 bpm

Andante: walking, 75 to 100 bpm

Moderato: moderate speed, 100 to 120 bpm

Allegro: fast (cheerful), 120 to 160 bpm

Vivace: lively, 150 to 170 bpm

Presto: very fast, 170 to 200 bpm

Prestissimo: as fast as possible, 200 or more bpm

Examples of rhythm include swing, folk, shuffle, merengue, pop, waltz, bossa nova, funk, heavy metal, country, bluegrass, and so on.

Many musicians learned to play by playing along with CDs and records, or using a software program like Band-in-a-Box or a simple metronome that keeps the tempo rigidly. If you play along with a recording, you may have to retune your guitar slightly until it is in tune with the music. There are different ways of "feeling the beat," which we won't go into here. It's enough that you get a grasp of the basic ideas of tempo and rhythm.

Written Music

As you've seen, we can write out music in tablature.

FIGURE 4-1:
Music in
tablature

Each line represents a string, and each number on a string represents a fret to use to play the note—a pretty good system for writing down tunes, you'd think. A version of this kind of music notation was used by Renaissance and medieval lute players for years.

The problem is, we can't easily use this kind of chart to show how long we should sound a note. One beat? Two beats? Three beats? How can you tell? While tablature is handy, it has its limitations.

So how do we solve that problem? We split the note up so that it lasts for different lengths of time—all of which are reflections of each other.

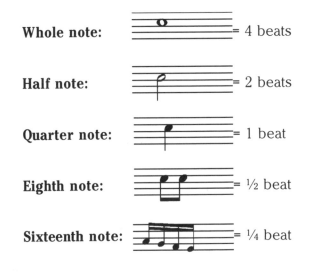

Whole note: = 4 beats

Half note: = 2 beats

Quarter note: = 1 beat

Eighth note: = ½ beat

Sixteenth note: = ¼ beat

You'll notice that notes below a quarter note have "flags" attached to the stem. The number of flags on a stem will tell us the kind of note we're playing.

Time Signatures

As we've seen already, we write 4/4 at the front of a piece (or sometimes 3/4, and so on). The top number (4 or 3) tells us how many beats in the bar to count. The bottom number tells us the kind of note we are counting (in this case, a quarter note). So if 4/4 means four quarter notes to each bar, and 3/4 means three quarter notes per bar, then 2/2—also known as *cut time*—would be what? You got it: two half notes to the bar. What would 6/8 be? Right: six eighth notes to the bar. And so on.

The notes in the bar have to add up to whatever the time signature says. For example, 3/4 would mean the notes must add up to three. Then a bar line | is drawn, and we start the next group of three. If the notes had to add up to four, then we would make sure there was a bar line every time the notes added up to four.

For example, these notes all add up to four:

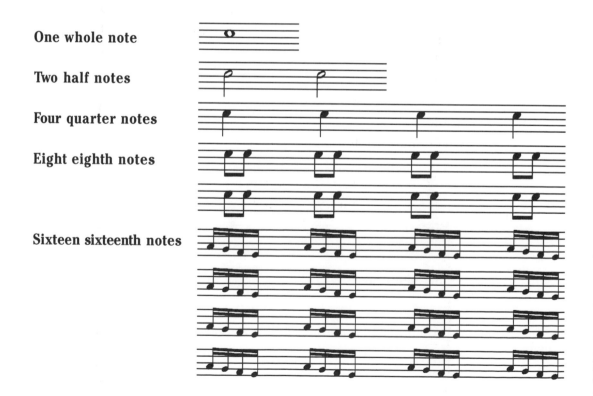

One whole note

Two half notes

Four quarter notes

Eight eighth notes

Sixteen sixteenth notes

These notes add up to three:

One half note and a quarter note

Three quarter notes

Six eighth notes

Twelve sixteenth notes

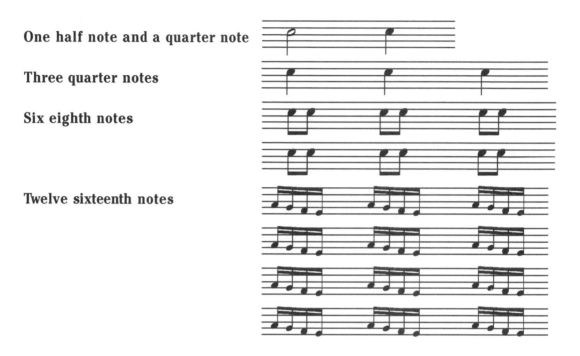

What if you don't want a note to be played? Or you want one note to last longer than usual? Each of the notes has a corresponding rest note, which indicates that you should not play for that brief period. So you could also make up beats by inserting a half note and a quarter note rest, or a half note rest and a quarter note, or two quarter notes and a quarter note rest, and so forth. See **FIGURE 4-2**.

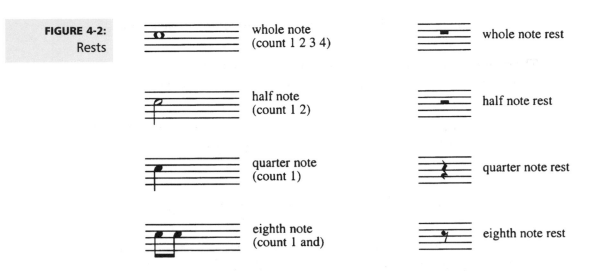

FIGURE 4-2:
Rests

whole note
(count 1 2 3 4)

whole note rest

half note
(count 1 2)

half note rest

quarter note
(count 1)

quarter note rest

eighth note
(count 1 and)

eighth note rest

If we write a dot immediately after a note, it will increase that note's duration by half as much again. For example, a dotted whole note would be four beats plus two, totaling six. A dotted half note would be two beats plus one, totaling three. A dotted quarter note would be one beat plus a half of a beat. (In this case, the next note would start on the "offbeat.")

Another way to make a note last longer—and keep everything neatly within the bar lines—is to tie two notes together. In **FIGURE 4-3** for example, notice you play the first note, keep your finger down and continue to count for the length of the second note that is tied to the first with a curved bar connecting the two notes.

FIGURE 4-3:
Tied notes

count   1 (2   3)   1   2   3   (1 2 3)

Basic Elements

There are only seven notes in the musical alphabet, and then they repeat themselves: C-D-E-F-G-A-B (then C again, which is considered an "octave" or eight notes higher than the first C you played). You can start the sequence on any note you like, but it still repeats after 7 notes. (For example, A-B-C-D-E-F-G-[A]; F-G-A-B-C-D-E-[F], etc.)

There are two basic elements to reading and writing music: the name of the note in the musical alphabet you want a musician to play; and how long that note should last. Over time, these two elements became combined into one elegant system—called *musical notation.* A five-line "staff" developed, and the note's position and appearance on the staff told musicians what note to play and how long to hold the note before playing the next note.

The modern staff is split into two halves, each of which is called a *clef,* and each of which has a particular sign at the beginning to tell us which staff we are using. These clefs are called the *treble clef* and the *bass clef.* When piano players read music, they play the treble clef with their right hand and the bass clef with their left hand.

Notes that appear below or above the clefs appear on what are called *ledger lines*—individual lines for each note—but we won't worry too much about them for the moment.

Look at **FIGURE 4-4**. Notice that in between the treble clef and the bass clef is one note on a ledger line. That note is called middle C because it is the note C and it falls in the middle of the two clefs. It is usually played on the guitar as the note on String 5, third fret. (Actually, Middle C should be an octave higher, but we won't bother with that now.)

FIGURE 4-4:
Middle C

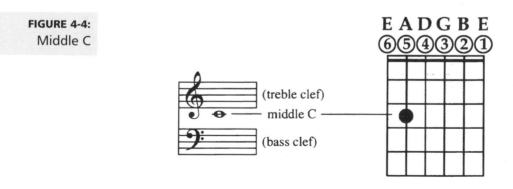

Because the notes on the lines and the spaces make up the musical alphabet in sequence, the note on the space after middle C will be D. The note on the next line will be E, on the next space F, and so on.

The great thing about the guitar is that you only have to learn the notes on the treble clef. If we look at all the notes on the lines, beginning with middle C, we see that they are:

FIGURE 4-5

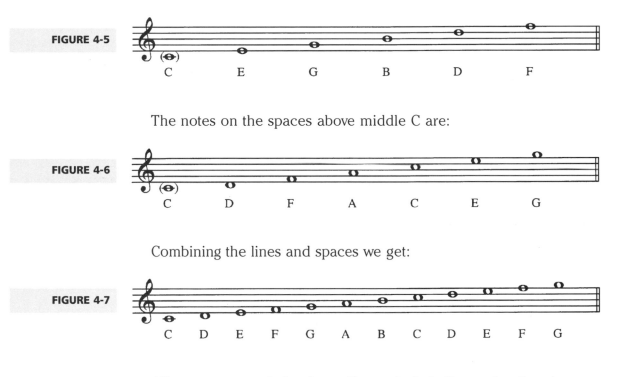

The notes on the spaces above middle C are:

FIGURE 4-6

Combining the lines and spaces we get:

FIGURE 4-7

All pretty easy and simple, really, particularly if you play the piano.

However, those of you who are quick off the mark may have figured out a little problem when it comes to playing the guitar. You may have noticed when you practice tuning up that you can play the same note (as it appears on the treble clef) in different places on the guitar. E, on the top space, for example, can be played on String 2, fifth fret, or on String 1, open. For the moment, we won't bother too much with this problem, as we're going to confine ourselves to reading music in the first position—that is, around the first fret. (Incidentally, the solution to the problem was developed by Segovia. Above the notes, you indicate the string you should use.)

Let's recap what we know, using notation.

FIGURE 4-8

Finding the Notes on the Guitar

Now we just need to find out where these notes are on the guitar. This section includes some exercises on the open strings that have fingerings to help you learn the musical alphabet.

FIGURE 4-9

(Bass Strings)

E ⑥ string   A ⑤ string   D ④ string

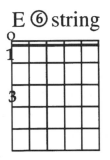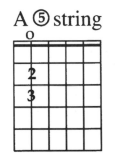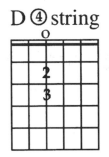

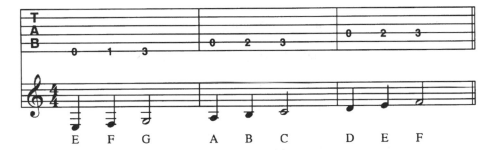

E F G   A B C   D E F

FIGURE 4-10

(Treble Strings)

G ③ string   B ② string   E ① string

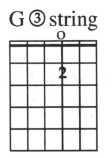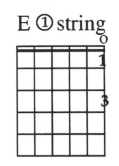

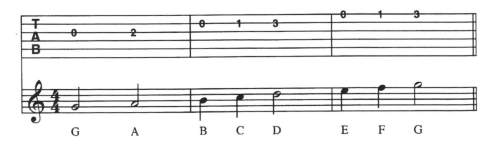

G A   B C D   E F G

Go back to some of the songs in the last two lessons and try reading the music now.

Dynamic Markings

When we talk about *dynamics,* we basically mean how loud or how soft you play the note or the chord. Again, the dynamic markings in music have Italian names. Here they are with their symbols:

pp:	pianissimo, very quietly
p:	piano, quiet
mp:	mezzo piano, moderately quiet
mf:	mezzo forte, moderately loud
f:	forte, loud
ff:	fortissimo, very loud

Staccato means "short and sharp." When you play staccato, you keep the rhythm of the piece, but you play the notes for a shorter duration than you normally would. Staccato notes are often marked with dots underneath.

The opposite of staccato is *legato,* which means "slurred." Here you slur the notes together, maybe playing one note and hammering down on the next note using left-hand fingering alone.

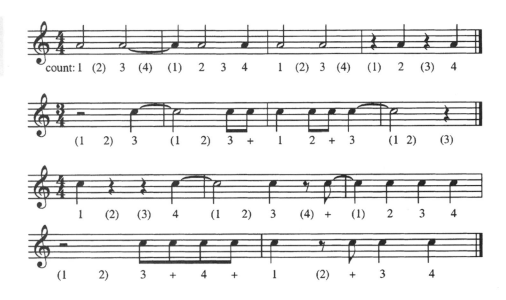

FIGURE 4-11:
Exercise in
counting notes

count: 1 (2) 3 (4) (1) 2 3 4   1 (2) 3 (4) (1) 2 (3) 4

(1) 2) 3   (1 2) 3 + 1 2 + 3   (1 2)   (3)

1 (2) (3) 4   (1) 2) 3 (4) + (1) 2 3 4

(1) 2) 3 + 4 + 1 (2) + 3 4

Key Signatures

As we've seen, notes can be on lines (E-G-B-D-F) or spaces (D-F-A-C-E-G) on the staff (sometimes also called a "stave"). We can also raise or lower these notes one fret or half step using sharp (♯) to raise and flat (♭) to lower. Instead of placing lots of sharps or flats into some tunes, we can instead put these sharps or flats at the beginning of a piece of music, which then tells us that all the notes that have a sharp or flat sign in front of them (as musicians describe it, the accidental is placed on the staff before the note or is "in front of it"). These notes should be played that way unless a natural sign (♮) tells you otherwise.

What's more, depending on how many sharps or flats there are at the beginning of a piece of music, we can tell which key the music is written in.

One flat = key of F
Two flats = key of B♭
Three flats = key of E♭
Four flats = key of A♭
Five flats = key of D♭
Six flats = key of G♭

Six flats (or altered notes) are just about as many notes as you need to remember. After this we get into what are "enharmonic" notes, or notes that have the same name, such as "C flat" which is really B natural. As a result, we usually start to think about sharp keys at this point.

Six sharps = key of F♯
Five sharps = key of B
Four sharps = key of E
Three sharps = key of A
Two sharps = key of D
One sharp = key of G
No sharps or flats = key of C

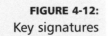

FIGURE 4-12:
Key signatures

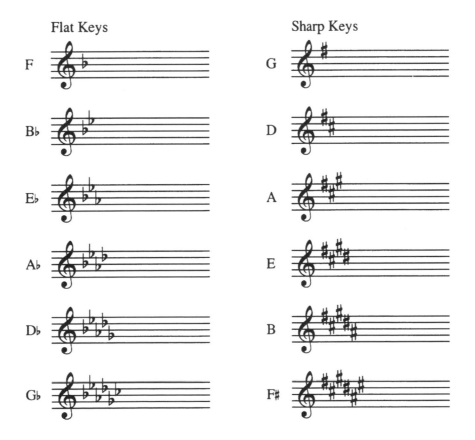

Flat Keys   Sharp Keys

When you're comfortable with all this, try these next couple of tunes.

FIGURE 4-13:
Polly Wolly
Doodle

Polly Wolly Doodle

FIGURE 4-14:
Drunken Sailor

Drunken Sailor

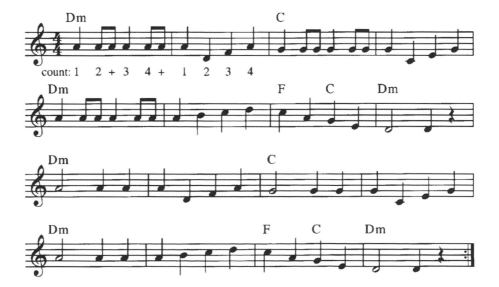

FIGURE 4-15:
We Wish You a
Merry Christmas

We Wish You a Merry Christmas

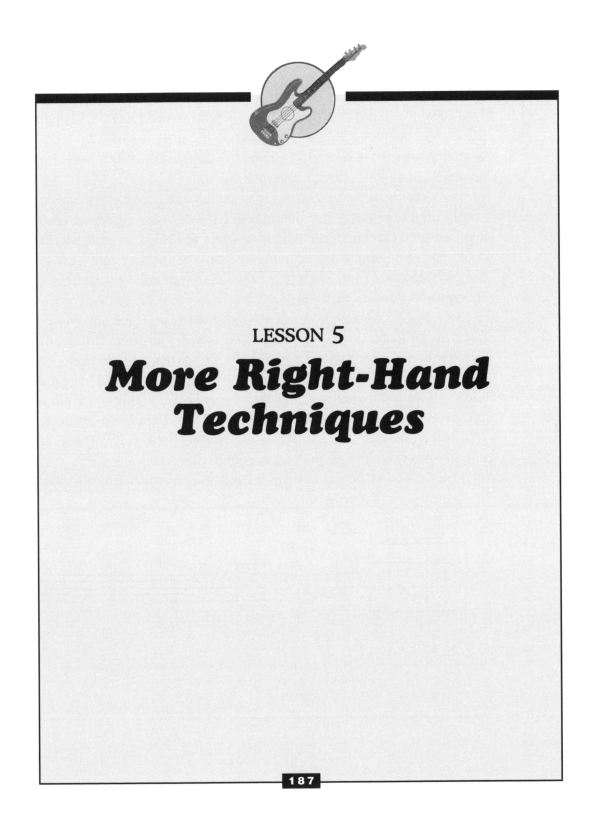

LESSON 5

More Right-Hand Techniques

Basic Rhythm Guitar

This lesson will help you explore some of the possibilities of playing the guitar by concentrating on what the right hand does. Right-hand technique is often the major element in defining the difference in style between genres such as folk, country, and rock-and-roll.

Let's start with some strumming or rhythm exercises using a pick.

Up until now you've just been playing downstrokes (unless you've been adventurous and tried to include some upstrokes as well). To this point, you've determined how many beats in the bar to count based on the time signature (4/4, 3/4, etc.). Now let's explore the possibilities of accents and different rhythms.

You should use a metronome for these exercises. Pick any chord—an E chord, for instance—and try these exercises. Try to keep time so well with the metronome that the sound of the "tick" disappears. Most important, try to make your time and chord changes as fluid as possible and as close to the metronome ticks as possible. If you flub the change, don't sweat it. Good time is more important here than good articulation. That will come with practice. If it helps, change between an E and an Ami chord every time there is an accent to play.

Now let's work on some rhythm guitar and accents. Try this exercise to develop your rhythm guitar playing:

FIGURE 5-1(a)

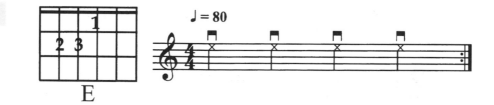

> An X indicates a rhythm beat, not a note to be played. It's how drummers write music for themselves. Remember, the symbol ⊓ means a downstroke. The symbol V means an upstroke.

FIGURE 5-1(b):
Rhythm exercises

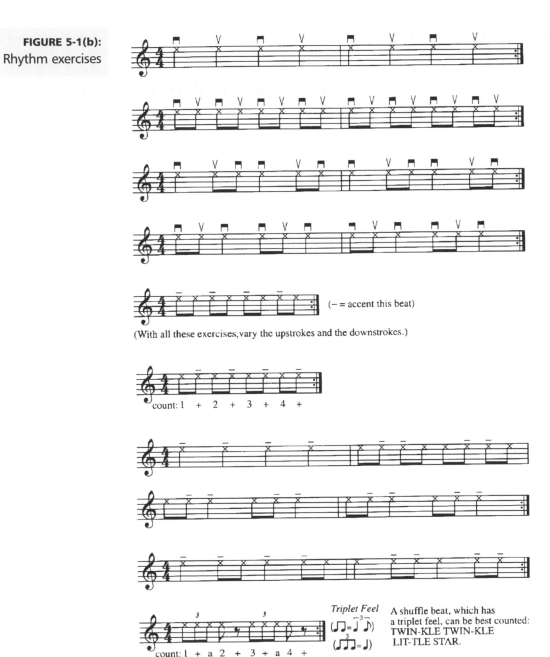

(— = accent this beat)

(With all these exercises, vary the upstrokes and the downstrokes.)

count: 1 + 2 + 3 + 4 +

count: 1 + a 2 + 3 + a 4 +

Triplet Feel

A shuffle beat, which has a triplet feel, can be best counted:
TWIN-KLE TWIN-KLE LIT-TLE STAR.

Basic Alternate Bass Picking

Play an E chord. Play String 6 open with your pick, and then strum the rest of the chord using a downstroke, like this:

FIGURE 5-2

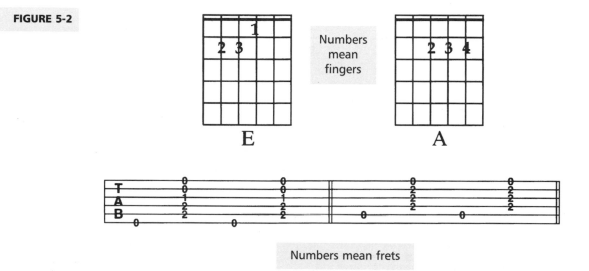

This "boom-chick" kind of sound is called *alternating bass.* Playing the bass note on String 6 for the E chord and then the bass note on String 5 for the A chord starts to develop a pattern.

Eventually, you can really develop long bass note runs this way, suggesting a bass player accompanying the guitar (or, if you prefer, the idea that you are playing left and right hands on a piano). However, to begin with, just keep things very simple, with one bass note per chord. The coordination needed to play like this and sing along is really hard, so don't get upset if it all falls apart the first few times you try this.

FIGURE 5-3:
Wabash
Cannonball

Wabash Cannonball

Basic Fingerpicking

There's a difference between classical right-hand position and folk and blues style right-hand positions, but the essence of the right-hand styles is the same.

FIGURE 5-4:
Right-hand
position

The right-hand thumb plays the three bass strings, the first finger plays the third string, the second finger plays the second string, and the third finger plays the first string. The stroke comes from the finger joint, not the knuckle.

FIGURE 5-5(a)

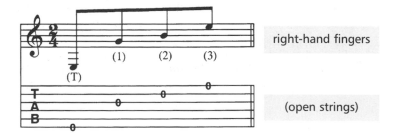

right-hand fingers

(open strings)

FIGURE 5-5(b)

For a good classical technique, its best to grow your nails slightly, so that you get a nice percussive attack, and slightly arch your wrist so that the fingers are vertical to the strings.

The difference between the hand position in folk/blues right-hand picking and classical guitar playing is one of degree. Note that while the folk/blues position seems more relaxed, it can also cause some muscle strain if you're not careful.

Go back and practice the early pick exercises using your fingers instead of the plectrum to play the treble strings.

Folk Picking

Now that you have some basic ideas about how the right hand can work, let's explore some right-hand finger patterns used in various forms of music. We'll start with folk music. As you learn new songs, experiment with these different right-hand patterns.

FIGURE 5-6(a)

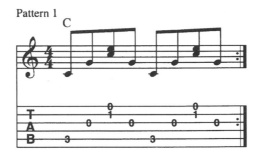

Pattern 1

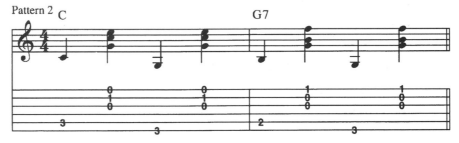

Pattern 2

Pattern 3

Pattern 4

FIGURE 5-6(b)

Pattern 5 "Carter Style"

(Play the notes with stems down with your thumb.)

Pattern 6 "Travis Style"

Step 1: Set up a bass pattern.

Step 2: Add a treble string, keeping the bass steady.

Step 3: Add a 2nd treble string, keeping the bass steady.

Step 4 (last step): Pinch the 1st string and 5th string together.

Notice that you use your thumb to play the bass notes. Also, pinch together a bass note and a treble string so that you can pick out the melody of a tune while giving the impression you're keeping a steady bass line going. This takes lots of practice but can sound really cool!

Basic Blues

The following illustration shows some basic blues rhythms to start you off.

FIGURE 5-7

The next one shows a twelve-bar shuffle blues rhythm in tab form.

FIGURE 5-8:
12-bar blues
in A

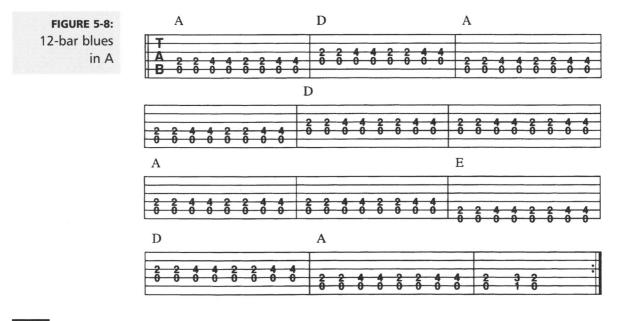

Country Picking

An advanced form of right-hand picking combines holding a pick and using the fingers at the same time.

FIGURE 5-9

It's pretty hard to do, but it's popular with country players and some jazz musicians who play solo guitar. Often it entails the unorthodox technique of using the little finger of the right hand, which is not used in any other fingerstyle technique.

LESSON 6

Beyond the Basics and Moveable Chord Shapes

The Whole Enchilada . . .

So far you've learned that the musical alphabet consists of seven letters: A-B-C-D-E-F-G. Actually, there are five other notes in the musical alphabet, although they are variations on the seven letters you already know.

Think back to the piano keyboard image we showed you in the section on tuning a guitar.

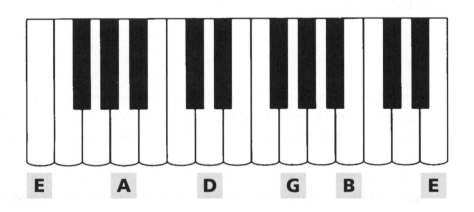

Did you notice that there were a number of white notes and black notes that weren't named? Let's fill in those spaces.

FIGURE 6-1:
Strings

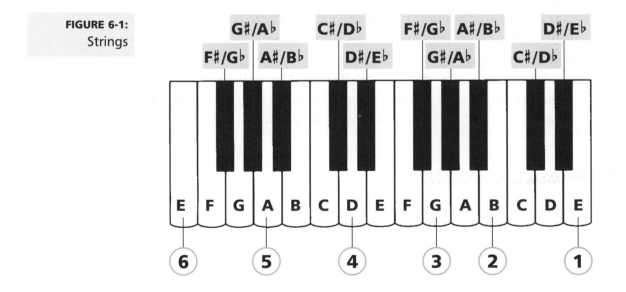

If you look carefully, you'll see that some notes have a ♯ (sharp) sign in front of them, and some have a ♭ (flat) sign in front of them. These notes are called *accidental notes*. Look again and you'll notice that the same note can be called either a sharp note or a flat note. How is that possible?

Baby Steps

In Western music (as opposed to music from the Middle East and the Far East), musical notes move in half-steps. These half-steps correspond to the keys on a piano. The black keys represent the sharp/flat keys, and the white keys represent the musical alphabet as you currently know it. Look really closely and you'll see that in two different places there are two white notes together. Otherwise, the keys alternate white notes with black notes.

Starting from E, there is a half-step between E and F. (This is the first pair of white notes that go together. We'll discuss this in the lesson on harmony.)

Between F and G there is a black note, which we can call either F♯ (F sharp), which is a half-step up from F, or G♭ (G flat), which is a half-step down from G. (F♯ and G♭ are said to be *enharmonic notes*— that is, they're the same.) Between G and A there is another black note, called G♯ or A♭ for the same reason; similarly between A and B is a note called either A♯ or B♭.

Between B and C there is a half-step. (This is the second pair of white notes that go together.) Between C and D is C♯ or D♭; and between D and E is D♯ or E♭. Then we're back to E again.

Chromatic Scale

All twelve notes together make up the musical alphabet and form what is called a *chromatic scale*. This is all you need to know to play and read music. See, we said it was easy.

As we've mentioned before, music is about what notes to play (melody), and how long you should play them (rhythm). The only other element you need to learn is harmony (which is what happens when you play two or more notes together at the same time). Again, we'll discuss this in the lesson on harmony.

Here is the complete chromatic scale moving in half-steps from the note E:

E, F, F♯/G♭, G, G♯/A♭, A, A♯/B♭, B, C, C♯/D♭, D, D♯/E♭, (E).

This is how it looks written out in standard musical notation:

FIGURE 6-2:
Chromatic scale

Note:
♯ = sharp
♭ = flat
♮ = natural (In front of a note, it means play the note without sharps or flats, i.e., naturally.)

Notice that in musical notation the sharp (♯) and flat (♭) signs come in front of the note. A natural sign (♮) in front of a note means that you play that note without making it sharp or flat—as it is naturally played.

How the Guitar Fits In

So how does the guitar fit in to all this? You may recall that we said each fret of the guitar is a half-step away from the next. So the guitar fretboard naturally forms a chromatic scale. Very useful.

If you play E, String 6, open, and then the note on every fret on the E string up to the twelfth fret, you will have played a chromatic scale starting on E. Try it.

If you play A, String 5, open, and then the note on every fret up to the twelfth fret, you will have played a chromatic scale starting on A, and so on.

The next figure shows all the notes on all the strings.

FIGURE 6-3

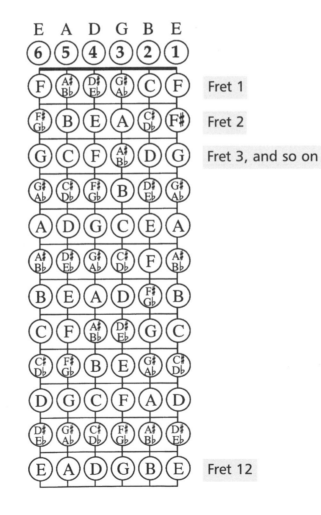

This is a really important concept, because now we can do lots of things on the guitar fretboard, not just confine ourselves to open-string chords. The most important thing we can do is move the same chord shape up and down the neck!

Moveable Chords

The idea that we can move one shape up and down the neck and play lots of chords at the same time is pretty amazing. These chords are called *moveable chords*.

You already know there are different types of chords. You've learned about major chords, minor chords, and seventh chords (also called *dominant seventh chords*). You've probably wondered how these different types of chords get their names. Why E, or C, or G7, or Ami? We'll go into this in more detail in the harmony chapter. For now, all you need to know is that a chord has a name (or root) note. This note is usually found somewhere on one of the three bass strings.

For example, the name (root) note of E is on String 6, open.

FIGURE 6-4

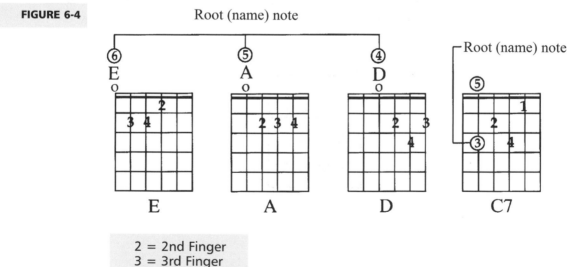

2 = 2nd Finger
3 = 3rd Finger
4 = little Finger

The name note or root note of A is found on String 5, open, and the name/root note of D is found—where? Right, on String 4, open.

Look at the last chord in the previous figure. It's a new chord, called C7. It gets its name from the note on the third fret on String 5. When you play it, don't play String 6 or String 1; just play the inner four strings.

Using the same fingering, move that chord shape up two frets. Your third finger, on String 5, should now be at the fifth fret, and your first finger should be on String 2 at the third fret. (The other two fingers should be in the same pattern as the diagram, obviously. We're moving shapes here, right?)

Remember, this chord gets its name from the note on String 5. Look at the chromatic scale, look at your fingers on the fretboard (you are trying to play this chord, right?), and try to figure out what the name of this chord should now be. The question is: What's the name of the note on String 5 at the fifth fret?

Moving a C7 chord shape from the first position (your first finger is playing a note on the first fret, get it?) to the third position (first finger is now playing a note on the third fret) means that the new chord is called D7.

"Wait a minute," we hear you cry. "Don't you play D7 a different way? In Lesson 3, you distinctly said a D7 chord should be played this way."

FIGURE 6-5

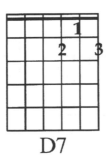

D7

You're absolutely right. In fact, you can play the same chord in different ways all over the guitar neck. (We'll talk about this in more detail later on.) Here's the thing: Play the D7 chord as you originally learned it. Now play it using the new shape you've just learned. It's the same chord, but somehow it sounds subtly different. So you now have a choice of ways to play D7, depending on how the chord sounds. Besides, with a little practice, you'll find that it's much easier to change from chord to chord using moveable shapes.

Barre Chords

Barre (pronounced *bar*) chords are a special kind of moveable chord. You create them by using your first finger to stop all the strings across a fret, and then you play a moveable shape under it. Don't panic; it's pretty easy, although it takes a little practice.

Practice this: Put your first finger across all six strings at the first fret. If you have trouble getting all the notes to sound clearly, put your second finger on top of your first to help press it down until the notes ring clearly. Relax. Flex your fingers. Now try it again. Move your first finger to the second fret, play the strings, then relax your hand. Repeat this at the third fret, and then the fourth—and so on—trying to get a clear sound from each note on the strings as you do it. Use that first finger to stop all the frets in turn as far up the neck as you can go, playing all the strings at a fret, relaxing your hand, and then trying again, all the time making sure that the notes on each string sound clear, and don't buzz or sound muffled. Like everything else with the guitar, it gets easy with a little practice.

Now look at the notes on String 6. If the root note, or name note, for the E major chord is String 6, open, then theoretically, if we move the "E shape" up one fret, we move the root note up one fret as well.

Use your first finger to barre the strings on the first fret. Use the suggested fingering to play an "E shape" chord at the first position/fret while you barre the first fret with your first finger. This is not easy, but persevere. Try to get all the notes on all the strings to sound clear when you play them. Relax your hand.

The note on the first fret of String 6 is F. That means that an "E shape" chord, which in the open-string position is called E, in the first position (that is, at the first fret) is called F. Move it up to the third fret and now it is called G.

Quick test—Try to find and play these chords:

G♭ (Major), F7, C♯7, A♭, E♭7, and F♯. (Hint: You'll find the root notes of all these chords on either String 6 or String 5.)

Having trouble with this exercise? Take a break, grab a cola or a coffee, and then reread this chapter until you're comfortable with the concept we're talking about and you can find these chords. It's really not that hard. Honest.

Go back through some of the earlier lessons and try playing the songs using the moveable chord shapes you've learned.

Moveable Shapes

FIGURE 6-6 shows moveable chord types gathered together based on the location of the root note. Some of these chords have fingerings that are not that easy because they involve using more than one finger to barre more than one fret—A, for instance, or Dmi7—but with a little practice, you'll get it.

FIGURE 6-6:
E-shape:
Major, Maj

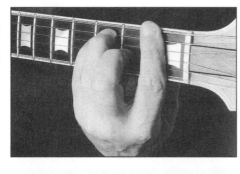

Maj

E-shape:
dominant 7,
7, dom7

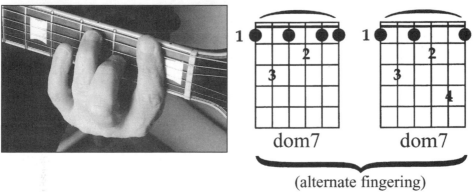

dom7   dom7

(alternate fingering)

E-shape:
minor, mi

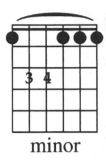

minor

E-shape:
minor7, mi7

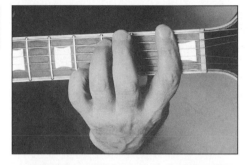

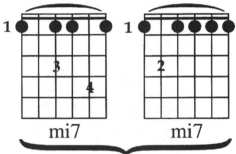

mi7   mi7

(alternate fingering)

A-shape:
Maj (double
barred chord)

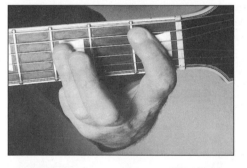

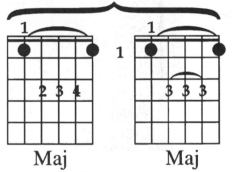

Maj   Maj

A-shape:
dom7

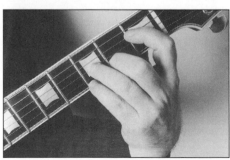

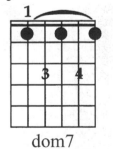

dom7

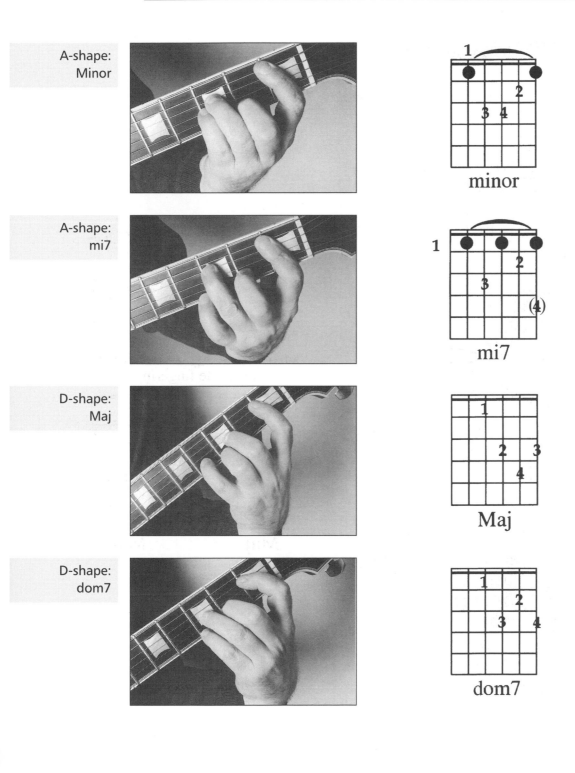

A-shape: Minor

minor

A-shape: mi7

mi7

D-shape: Maj

Maj

D-shape: dom7

dom7

D-shape:
mi

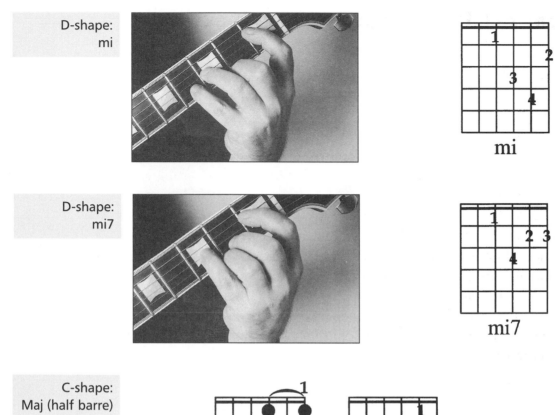

mi

D-shape:
mi7

mi7

C-shape:
Maj (half barre)

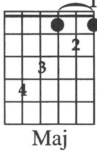

Maj   dom7

Moveable Chords with Muted Notes

Up until now we've haven't made much of a fuss about which strings you strum when you finger a chord. It's been enough that you get the strings to sound out clearly without buzzing or making some other noise while you fret the notes and play.

At the beginning of this lesson, we asked you to play a C7 chord. We also said, "*Don't play* String 6 and String 1, just the middle four strings." What we did, in a way, is mute or deaden the sound of String 6 and String 1 so that they wouldn't sound when you played the chord. That's because while the open note E is part of a C7 chord, if you move that chord shape up the neck, the note E quickly clashes with the other "C7 shape" chords that you play that *don't* contain the note E in them. We'll explain more about why this is important in the lesson on harmony.

A *muted chord* is one in which you must deaden (or mute) one or two strings while you play the chord. You mute the strings so that you get the correct *key tones* out of the chord shape every time you play it, wherever you play it.

FIGURE 6-7

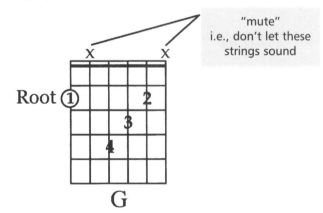

"mute"
i.e., don't let these
strings sound

Root ①

G

This figure shows a moveable G chord with two strings (that is, notes) crossed out with an *x*: String 5 and String 1. That means you shouldn't let these strings sound when you play the chord. A pretty tall order, right? Even knowing about barre chords, haven't we just spent a whole book saying you should make the notes ring out clearly? Well, the answer is yes—and no. As you get better at playing the guitar, you'll find that some things that are good to do when you're beginning are not so good to do when you become more advanced.

To mute a string, you need to shape your hand in such a way that these two strings are dampened or deadened when you strum a downstroke. To sound the note, we've told you to use the tip of your finger on your left hand. To dampen or mute a note, use the "fatty" or flat part of either the side of your finger or just under your fingertip, depending on the kind of chord you're trying to play. Now play each of the remaining notes of the chord until they sound clear. Play them individually (called an *arpeggio*) to make sure you have them right.

Here are the five basic seventh chords in muted forms:

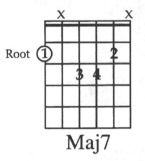

Maj7

dom7

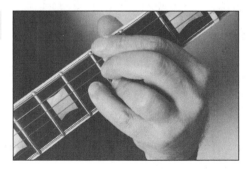

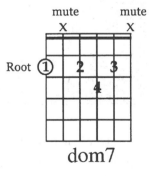

dom7

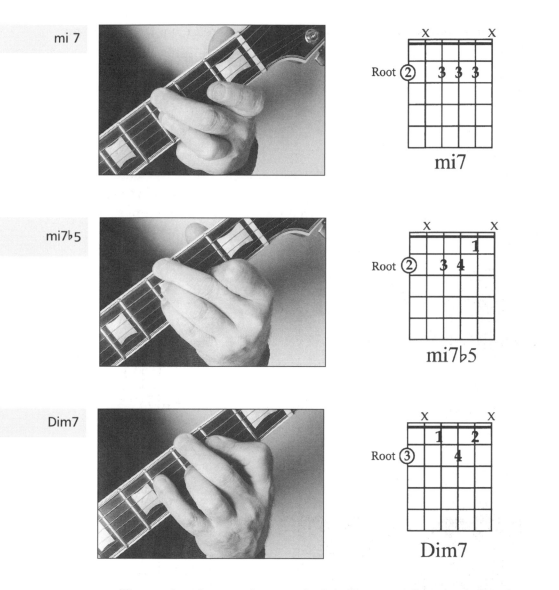

mi 7

mi7♭5

Dim7

These chords sound very colorful. If you can learn to play them well, you'll develop a great feeling of achievement.

We don't have the room here to really explore this whole concept of moveable chords and muted chords, but there are lots of books out there on the subject, a few of which are listed in the appendix. Here we've tried to give you an idea of how this works, and show you how you can go forward if it's something that appeals to you.

LESSON 7

Playing in Position

Position Playing

Well, you've come along quite a ways! By the time you've mastered the concept of moveable chords and the material in this chapter, playing in position, you'll be able to think of yourself as an intermediate player.

Up until now we've pretty much covered the basic things you can do using the open strings, or as it is more accurately called, in the open position. The simplest way to think of position playing is to think about where your first finger lies on the guitar neck. We talked about left-hand fingering in Lesson 3. You tried an exercise in which each finger of the left hand had a fret it covered. The first finger played notes on the first fret, the second finger played notes on the second fret, the third finger played notes on the third fret, and the fourth finger played notes on the fourth fret.

Strictly speaking, to play a chromatic scale we should only play three notes on String 3 because the fourth fret (B) is the same note as String 2, open (B), and there's no need to repeat. So try the chromatic scale again using the proper fingering.

FIGURE 7-1:
Chromatic scale fingering

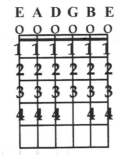

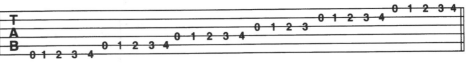

Using the open strings, we are playing in the open position. If we start this exercise on F (first fret String 6) and play it as shown in the following figure, then we are playing in the first position, because that is where the first finger is lying on the guitar fretboard.

FIGURE 7-2:
1st position
chromatic scale

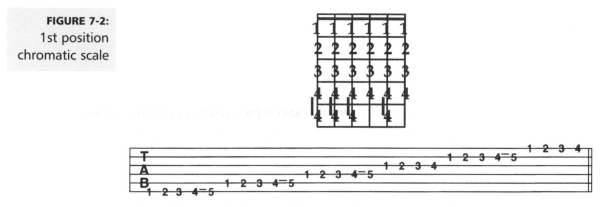

(Note: Slide your 4th finger up 1 fret to play the notes on the 5th fret.)

Let's explore this idea a bit more. The idea of position playing changes how we look at the guitar fretboard. Up until now, we've been thinking about moving around the guitar fingerboard as going up and down the neck vertically—say from the first fret to the second, third, fourth, and so on—moving chord shapes from one fret to another in order to get different chords. The problem here is that you can end up jumping all over the neck trying to play two chords or notes one after the other. There ought to be a more efficient way of doing things— and there is.

FIGURE 7-3

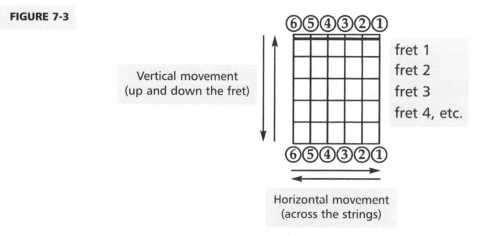

In position playing, we're starting to think about playing within the same number of frets but moving horizontally *across* the fingerboard—that is, from String 6 to String 1) so your fingers aren't jumping all over the neck looking for notes and chords. This is another really important concept.

Playing a Scale

Let's move to the second position. That means the first finger will play all the notes on the second fret, and the other fingers will play the next four frets (second finger plays third fret, third finger plays fourth fret, fourth finger plays fifth fret).

Let's play a C major scale in position. Look at the next figure. Notice the fingering. Even though the first note C is played on the third fret with the second finger, we're still in the second position because of where the first finger is.

FIGURE 7-4:

C major scale in 2nd position

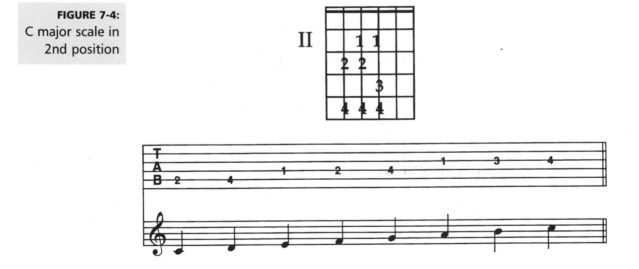

One of the great things about playing in position is that it becomes much easier to read music. It may seem that the easiest place to read music on the guitar is in the open position, but really, only the first four notes on String 6 have to be played in this position. Everything else can be played somewhere else.

Try this example. Let's get really adventurous and play in the seventh position. (Remember, that means the first finger covers notes on the seventh fret.)

Look at the following figure and play the scale.

FIGURE 7-5

Notice that the Roman numeral VII means the VII fret (7th fret).

FIGURE 7-6(a)

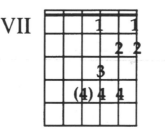

We can also extend the scale and play it again (making two octaves). Look at the fingering.

FIGURE 7-6(b)

VII

We can also extend the scale and play it again (making two octaves). Look at the fingering.

Moveable Patterns

Wait a minute, didn't we just play that? Indeed we did. It's the C major scale, this time starting on String 6 at the eighth fret. But wait a second—the finger pattern was the same as in the second position.

That's the trick about position playing. Because you aren't using open strings, you can really concentrate on a pattern of fingering and then move that pattern around the fingerboard, producing predictable results. If you learn, for example, that the fingering pattern for a major scale is 2–4, 1–2–4, 1–3–4, then you can play any major scale you like on String 6 and String 5. All you need to know is the name of the starting note.

But Wait, There's More . . .

If we play in the second position we can easily play the notes E, F, G♭, G, and A♭ on String 6, but we can only play up to the note A on String 1, fifth fret, comfortably. That means if you have to read a piece of music that doesn't have a note higher than this range, the best place to play the music would be in the second position.

FIGURE 7-7

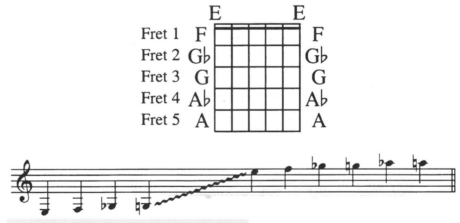

The range of notes in the 2nd position.

Look at "Daisy, Daisy." You can see that the highest note you have to play is A on the second fret, String 3, while the lowest note is A on String 5, open. So we can play the piece in the second position.

FIGURE 7-8:
Daisy, Daisy

Daisy, Daisy

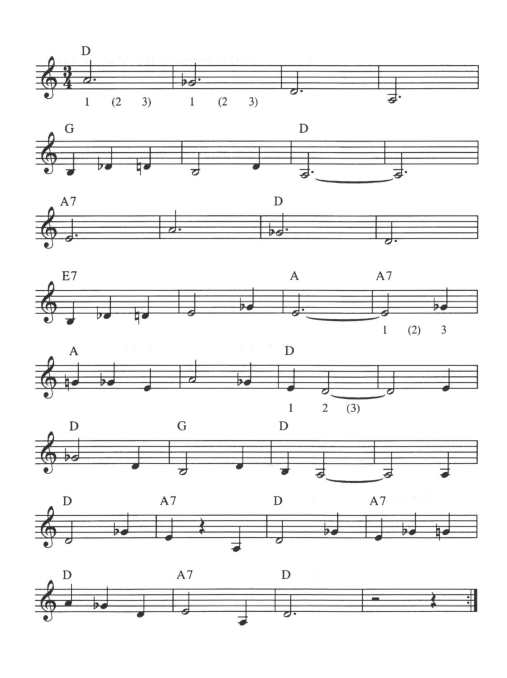

Now let's try playing in the seventh position. It's really easy. The only notes you haven't learned yet are the notes on String 1 starting on the fifth fret—A, B♭, B, C, D♭, D.

FIGURE 7-9

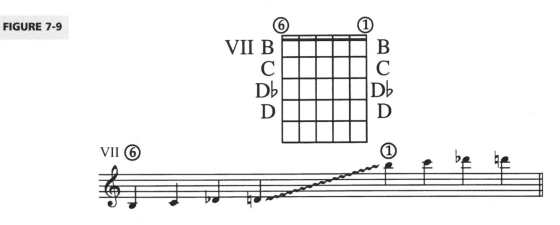

Here's the written range.

Now try the next exercise.

FIGURE 7-10:
7th position
exercise

Shifting Position

Of course, music doesn't have to be played in just one position—and it really shouldn't be. Very often we start in one position and then shift to another position, using what is called a *position shift*. Basically, all this means is that you move your first finger to a new place on the neck and the other fingers just naturally follow along.

Key Centers

You learned earlier that when we move the position of a chord, it becomes a different chord. For example, if we move an "E shape" chord to the fifth fret (fifth position), we're really playing an A chord. We can take that idea a little further here, by thinking of the fourth and fifth position as a good place to play chords, improvise solos, and so forth in the key of A. You'll need to experiment with this idea, but trust us, it works. (Move one fret higher and suddenly you are playing in the key of B♭.)

Similarly, you can play in the key of G at the second and third positions, or the key of C at the seventh and eighth positions. It also means that unusual keys like B♭, F♯, D♭, or B are really exactly the same as G or C or D, they're just at a different fret position. With a minimum of effort, you can suddenly play in any key, as long as you know the best position in which to play the key. Just remember, the first finger is the guide to moving the hand around the fingerboard, either vertically or horizontally.

LESSON 8

Basic
Harmony

What Is Harmony?

Harmony is such a vast subject people can study it the whole of their musical career without ever reaching the end. It's fascinating, and if you let it, it can take you on a journey from the rural Delta blues of Mississippi to the songs of the Beatles; from the rock and string compositions of Frank Zappa to the jazz composition and arrangements of Duke Ellington, Fletcher Henderson, Charlie Parker, John Coltrane, and George Russell; from the jigs and reels of Scotland and Ireland to the vast continent of classical music composition by such composers as John Dowland, Beethoven, Bach, Debussy, Stravinsky, Vaughan Williams, John Cage, and many, many more.

Yet at the root of all these vast and differing ways to make music are the same basic ideas: melody, rhythm, and harmony. We've already looked at melody, which is when notes follow each other to make up a tune; and rhythm, which is basically about how long the notes should be played, and how often. Now, we'll look at the third element, harmony, which is what happens when you play two or more notes together at the same time.

Yes, it's true that anything sounds good (at least to the composer) if you believe in it. However, most people expect music to sound a certain way, and as a result there are "rules" about how, when, and why certain notes should go together. Even if you're a punk headbanger, a John Cage fan, or into some other form of experimental music, to really stretch the envelope it's best that you have some understanding of the rules you're about to break.

And frankly, there are still questions we can't answer. We can tell you, for example, *what* a major chord or a minor chord is, but we can't tell you *why* it's called a major chord or a major scale. Some things, it's best you just accept—at least for a while.

What we are going to look at applies equally to all the keys—to any key, in fact. But to make it easier to understand, we're going to look at everything in the key of C. The key of C does not naturally have any sharps or flats (accidentals), so the variations and so forth can be more easily seen.

Here is the scale of C major. Notice that the notes fall alternately on lines and spaces. For example, C is on a ledger line, D is on a space, E is on a line, F is on a space, and so on.

FIGURE 8-1:
C major scale

C   D   E   F   G   A   B   C

Intervals

Let's start with the concept of the distance between two notes, which is called an *interval.* You'll remember that we said the frets of a guitar are a half-step or half-tone apart (same thing, different name). Well, a half-tone or semitone (same thing, different name) is the smallest interval, or distance, between two notes—at least in Western music. This is the distance from C to C♯. (C♯ is one half-step *up from C*, remember, and D♭ is enharmonically the same note, a half-step *down from D.*)

A whole step or whole tone (usually just called a *tone*), which is two semitones, would be from C to D. This would be the equivalent of jumping to a note two frets away on the guitar.

It's very helpful not only to know this information intellectually, but also to see how you can apply it to your instrument. Look at the fingerboard.

The distance from C, third fret, String 5 to C♯, fourth fret, String 5 is a semitone.

The distance from C, third fret, String 5 to D, fifth fret, String 5 is a whole tone.

Intervals by Semitone

From C to D♭ is a minor second—that is, one semitone.

From C to D is a second—that is, two semitones.

From C to E♭ is a minor third—three semitones.

From C to E is a major third—four semitones.

From C to F is a fourth—five semitones.

From C to G♭ is a diminished or flattened fifth—six semitones.
If we say the interval is from C to F♯ (enharmonically the same note as G♭, remember), this can be called an augmented fourth. *Flattening*—or *diminishing*—a note means dropping it down a semitone or fret. *Augmenting* a note means sharpening or raising it a semitone or fret.

From C to G is a fifth—seven semitones.

From C to G♯ is an augmented fifth (also called a *raised* fifth)—eight semitones. In the same way as before, C to A♭ (enharmonically the same note) is a minor sixth.

From C to A is a major sixth—nine semitones.

From C to A♯ is an augmented sixth—ten semitones.
In the same way, from C to B♭ is a minor seventh—ten semitones.

From C to B is a major seventh—eleven semitones.

From C to C is an octave—twelve semitones.

FIGURE 8-2:
Intervals written
as notation

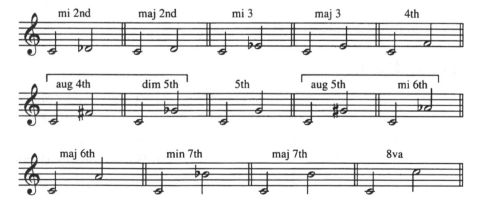

Scales

Both major scales and minor scales are created by putting together a series of tones and semitones. Of course, depending on whether the scale is major or minor, these tones and semitones are arranged in a different sequence.

Major Scale

There are lots of good books on harmony, and it's not necessary now to know all the theory that goes into creating scales. If you're interested, you should take a look in the appendix for some books you can start with.

If we look at the major scale again, we can see it is built this way:

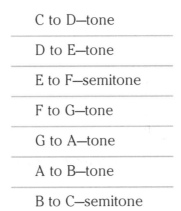

C to D—tone

D to E—tone

E to F—semitone

F to G—tone

G to A—tone

A to B—tone

B to C—semitone

So the pattern for a major scale is tone, tone, semitone, tone, tone, tone, semitone.

Minor Scale

Each major scale has a corresponding minor scale (called the *relative minor*), built on the sixth note of the major scale. There are three different types of minor scales that we can study: the harmonic minor, the melodic minor, and the natural minor. Each scale is built slightly differently from the other.

The natural minor scale is the easiest to start with because it's composed of all the notes of the related major scale (in this case, C), starting on the sixth note of the scale.

FIGURE 8-3

C major scale

A natural minor scale
(starts on 6th of C scale)

A harmonic minor scale consists of tone, semitone, tone, tone, semitone, minor third, semitone.

FIGURE 8-4

A harmonic minor scale

C harmonic minor scale

In the key of A minor, it would be called A harmonic minor:

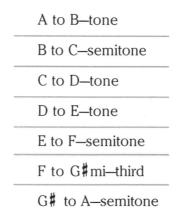

A to B—tone

B to C—semitone

C to D—tone

D to E—tone

E to F—semitone

F to G♯mi—third

G♯ to A—semitone

In the key of C it would be C harmonic minor, and would be built this way: C-D-E♭-F-G-A♭-B-C.

A melodic minor scale is more complex because it is often played in classical harmony as ascending in one form and descending in another. However, for our purposes we'll learn it the same way going up and down.

The melodic minor is built of tone, semitone, tone, tone, tone, tone, semitone. In the key of A melodic minor it would be A-B-C-D-E-F♯-G♯-A.

In the key of C melodic minor it would be C-D-E♭-F-G-A-B-C.

FIGURE 8-5

A melodic minor scale

C melodic minor scale

Chord Structures

The combination of three or more notes is a chord. Three note chords are called *triads*. Four note chords are called *seventh chords*.

Triads

There are four types of triads: major, minor, augmented, and diminished, which are built by piling major thirds and minor thirds on top of each other in different combinations. You can "spell" the four triad chords this way:

C maj	C-E-G	maj 3rd min 3rd
C mi	C-E♭-G	min 3rd maj 3rd
C aug	C-E-G♯	maj 3rd maj 3rd
C dim	C-E♭-G♭	mi 3rd mi 3rd

Most chord structures are a variation on these four triads.

The following figure gives you an example of how these triads can be played on the guitar.

FIGURE 8-6: Triads

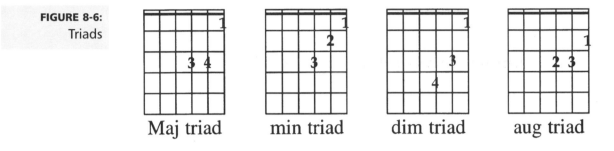

On the guitar, these simple chords are not usually spelled this way. For example, you can mix up the order of the notes, and instead of playing C-E-G, you can play G-C-E. You can also double notes. An E maj triad is spelled E-G♯-B, for example, but it is usually played E-B-E-G♯-B-E.

It's not really important now to know these structures inside out. Instead, learn the chord forms on the chord diagrams. Try to figure out where other triads can be played on the guitar and write them down for yourself.

Seventh Chords

Four-note chords are called seventh chords. They generally have much more color and sound more interesting than triads. Furthermore, they are the basis of all our standard repertoire of tunes. To make a seventh chord, add either a major third or a minor third to one of the four triad forms. Doing this, we get five basic seventh chords, with other chords being variations on these five.

In the key of C, the five are:

C maj7	C-E-G-B	
C7	C-E-G-B♭	(also called a dominant 7)
C mi7	C-E♭-G-B♭	
C mi7♭5	C-E♭-G♭-B♭	(also written C¤7 or C half diminished)
C dim7	C-E♭-G♭-A	(the last note is usually called B double flat, but we'll call it A, which enharmonically it is)

As you've seen, we can make chords up by piling thirds on top of each other. Another way to look at chords is to build them from the tones of a scale (major or minor—it doesn't matter).

Here's a C major scale again:	C	D	E	F	G	A	B	C
Let's put numbers underneath:	1	2	3	4	5	6	7	8
Let's use Roman numerals:	I	II	III	IV	V	VI	VII	VIII

A chord can be built by choosing every other note in the scale and then altering it if necessary:

Cmaj7	1-3-5-7
C7	1-3-5-♭7
Cmi7	1-♭3-5-♭7
Cmi7♭5	1-♭3-♭5-♭7
Cdim7	1-♭3-♭5-♭♭7

Again, while on the piano keyboard it is easier to play these chords as we've spelled them out here, on the guitar that isn't the case. A Cmaj7 chord, for example, is often played on the guitar spelled C-G-B-E, or C-B-E-G.

If you spend some time working on understanding how chords are built, you'll soon be able to build your own. For example, if you know how to play a Cmaj7 chord, and suddenly you are confronted with Cmaj7♯5, you just need to play a Cmaj7 shape, figure out which note is the fifth of the chord, and raise it up a fret (semitone) to make the ♯5 part of this chord. (The chord, of course, would be spelled 1-3-♯5-7—that is, in the key of C: C-E-G♯-B.)

We said earlier that there are five basic seventh chords. That's true, but there are seven more chords that are variations on these five. Here are the twelve:

Cmaj7	1-3-5-7
C7	1-3-5-♭7
Cmi7	1-♭3-5-♭7
Cmi7♭5	1-♭3-♭5-♭7
Cdim7	1-♭3-♭5-♭♭7(6)
Cmaj7♯5	1-3-♯5-7
Cmaj7♭5	1-3-♭5-7
C7♯5	1-3-♯5-♭7
C7♭5	1-3-♭5-♭7
Cmi Maj7	1-♭3-5-7 (C minor Major 7)
C6	1-3-5-6
Cmi6	1-♭3-5-6

Think about this—a mi6 chord, and a mi7♭5 chord are the same thing, although they will have different root notes: Cmi6 = Ami7♭5.

Arpeggios

An arpeggio is simply a "broken" chord. In other words, if you play individually the notes that make up a chord—say Cmaj7, (C-E-G-B)—you are playing a Cmaj7 arpeggio. To play these arpeggios properly, you should learn them in two octaves. For example, C-E-G-B-C, E-G-B-C.

Single-note arpeggio practice (meaning playing one note of a chord at a time) is a wonderful way of getting these sounds in your head. It's also a terrific basis for learning how to improvise over a chord sequence.

Diatonic Chords

If you go through a major scale, building chords on every note of the scale by using every other note, you get what we call *diatonic chords*—all the chords that naturally occur in the key.

In the key of C, these are Cmaj7, Dmi7, Emi7, Fmaj7, G7, Ami7, Bmi7♭5, Cmaj7.

If you go through a harmonic minor scale, you get this sequence:

Cmi Maj7	Dmi7♭5	E♭maj7♯5	Fmi7	G7	A♭maj7	Bdim7	Cmi Maj7
I	II	III	IV	V	VI	VII	VIII

Standard Progressions

What we mean by *standard* here is "generally accepted" or "normal." There are standard tunes like "Over the Rainbow," "Moon River," and even "Happy Birthday to You" that are created using certain *chord progressions,* which means that a chord naturally progresses to another chord after it's played. (A G7 chord for example, naturally progresses to a Cmaj7, partly because G is the fifth note in the scale and key of C.)

If you go back and look at the seventh chords in the key of C, each has a Roman numeral under it. There's a reason for this. Instead of saying Cmaj7-Fmaj7-G7, for example, we could just say I IV V. Then we could look at the notes of *any* major scale, and play the I IV and V chords built on the first, fourth, and fifth notes of the scale. (They would be a maj7, maj7, dom7 sequence of chords.)

Cycle of Fourths and Fifths

If you go back to Lesson 4 and look at the section on key signatures, you may notice something now. If you follow the key signatures carefully, you'll see that from C to F is a fourth, and from F to B♭ is a fourth, and so on through the flat keys. Similarly, C to G is a fifth, G to D is a fifth, D to A is a fifth, and so on through the sharp keys. In fact, a fourth in one direction is a fifth in the other.

FIGURE 8-7:
Cycle of 4th
and 5ths

Cycle of 4th and 5ths

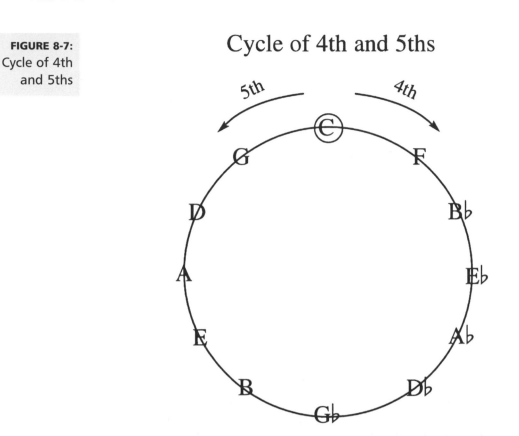

You've seen that we can use Roman numerals instead of chords. Following the flat keys (the notes that are a fourth away from each other), we get a series of V I chords. That is, C7 resolves to Fmaj7; F7 resolves to B♭maj7; B♭7 resolves to E♭maj7; E♭7 resolves to A♭maj7; A♭7 resolves to D♭maj7; D♭7 resolves to G♭maj7; G♭7 resolves to Bmaj7; B7 resolves to Emaj7; E7 resolves to Amaj7; A7 resolves to Dmaj7; D7 resolves to Gmaj7; and G7 resolves to C.

Practice this sequence using muted and moveable chords.

The Blues

To finish, let's look at a fun and usable progression: the blues. A blues sequence is really just a I IV V sequence. So a blues in B♭, say, would be B♭maj7, E♭maj7, F7.

Here's a basic twelve-bar blues in C (using triads):

```
4/4   C / / / | F / / / | C / / / |       |
      F / / / |         | C / / / |       |
      G / / / |         | C / / / |      ||
```

However, this is kind of bland and could use some color. Let's use dominant seven chords.

```
4/4   C7 / / / | F7 / / / | C7 / / / |      |
      F7 / / / |          | C7 / / / |      |
      G7 / / / |          | C7 / / / |     ||
```

A slightly more complicated sequence is called I VI II V. This sequence is the basis of most standard tune chord progressions. Using the diatonic chords you learned about earlier, in the key of C this would be Cmaj7, Ami7, Dmi7, G7. If you analyze songs by figuring out their key signatures, you'll discover that this I IV II V sequence is used in a lot of them.

One of the things you may well discover is that the root notes in the VI II V I sequence are all a fourth apart. (In key of C: A to D to G to C.) Next time you play a song, look for this pattern and this sequence. The more you practice using this cycle of fourths, the easier playing standard song progressions becomes.

Try this jazzy blues sequence:

```
4/4   C7 / / /    | F7 / F♯dim7 / | C7 / / / | Gmi7 / C7 / |
      F7 / / /    | F♯dim7 / / /  | C7 / / / | A7♯5 / / /  |
      Dm7 / / / | G7 / / /        | C7 / / / | (G7♯5 / / /) ||
```

When you practice chords and scales, try to practice them in the cycle of fourths sequence. First, play a C major scale, then an F major scale, then a B♭ major scale, and so on.

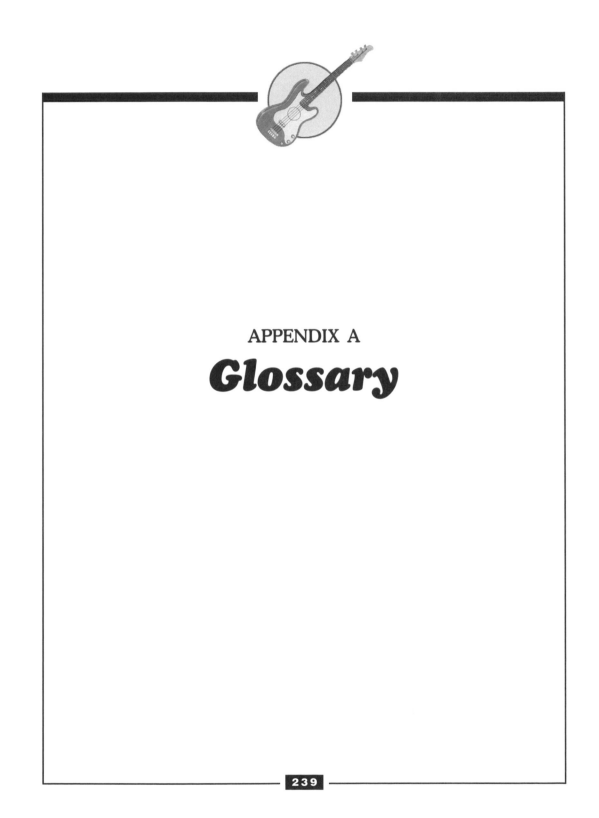

APPENDIX A

Glossary

accent: A dynamic effect that places an emphasis on a note or chord.

accidentals: Symbols in written music to raise (♯ - sharpen) or lower (♭- flatten) notes by semitones. A double flat (♭♭) lowers the pitch by a tone. A natural (♮) cancels the accidental alteration.

acoustic guitar: A hollow-bodied guitar that does not require electronic amplification.

action: The strings' playability along the neck. Action is affected by the strings' distance from the neck, the neck straightness, and the string gauge.

altered chord: A chord or scale in which one or more of the notes is changed to a note not normally associated with that scale.

archtop: A guitar, often an acoustic, with a curved top (soundboard) and F-holes similar to a violin's.

arpeggio: Literally, "like a harp"—that is, playing the notes of a chord one after the other rather than together. Also known as a *broken chord*.

artificial harmonics: Harmonics produced by fingering a note on the frets and lightly touching the string a fourth higher.

atonal: Not part of the tonal system of major and minor keys; in no key at all.

augmented (see also *diminished*)**:** Intervals increased by a semitone are known as *augmented intervals*. The augmented chord is a major chord with the fifth raised a semitone.

barre: A special kind of moveable chord created by stopping all the strings across a fret with your first finger and playing a moveable shape under it.

bebop, hard bop: A style of jazz that emerged in the 1940s, using fast melodic lines over adventurous extended harmonies, The terms *bop* and *bebop* are interchangeable, and *hard bop* usually refers to the 1950s blues-influenced variant.

binding: Thin strips of wood or plastic that seal the edges of the body.

blues: An African-American style of music that uses a scale including flattened thirds, fifths, and sevenths, known as the "blue notes" in a scale. A blues style has a predominantly twelve-bar form.

body: The main part of the guitar, to which the bridge and neck are attached. On acoustic guitars and some electrics, the body serves as a resonating chamber.

boogie-woogie: A style of blues and jazz with a repetitive rhythmic bass figure derived from early jazz piano-playing.

bossa nova: A Brazilian rhythmic style of jazz and popular music widespread in the United States and Europe in the 1960s.

bottleneck guitar: A technique using a metal bar or tube rather than the fingers of the left hand to play notes and chords, and to slide from one to another.

braces: Interior wooden strips that strengthen a hollow-bodied guitar. Brace size and configuration partly determine a guitar's tone.

break: In jazz, a short solo passage without accompaniment that usually occurs at the end of a phrase.

bridge: The structure that holds the saddle (or saddles), over which strings pass on the guitar body. Most bridges can be adjusted to raise or lower string height, changing the guitar's action and intonation.

C

capo: A spring-loaded, adjustable clamp that becomes in effect a "moveable nut." It fits over the neck and covers all the strings at a given fret, raising the pitch of the strings and allowing a singer or flamenco player to play in a different key and still use open-string chords and fingering.

chamber music: Music for small groups of players (usually no more than nine). The term *chamber jazz* is sometimes used for the more formal style of small combo such as the Modern Jazz Quartet.

changes: The sequence of chords used as a basis for improvisation in jazz.

choking: Damping the strings of the guitar to give short staccato chords.

chords: Any combination of three notes played together, usually based on the triad formed by the first, third, and fifth notes of the scale. For example, the chord of C major consists of C (the root of the chord), E, and G. Chords can be in root position—that is, with the root as the bass note—or various inversions using other notes in the chord as the bass.

chord substitutions: In jazz, alternatives to the conventionally used chords in a sequence.

chorus: On an electric guitar, simulates the effect of more than one instrument playing the same note.

chromatic: Chromatic notes are those that fall outside the notes of the key a piece of music is in. The chromatic scale is a twelve-note scale moving in semitones.

classical: The term *classical* is used loosely to describe art music to distinguish it from folk, jazz, rock, pop, and so forth, but more precisely it refers to the period of music from around 1750 through 1830.

comping: Jazz jargon for *accompanying*.

compression: On an electric guitar, boosts the volume of quieter notes, and reduces that of louder ones, evening out the sound of fast passages.

counterpoint, contrapuntal: The playing of two or more tunes at the same time, within the same harmonic framework. The added tunes are sometimes called *countermelodies*.

country (and Western): A predominantly white, rural popular music originally from the Southern and Western United States.

cutaway: An indented area of the body that allows the guitarist's fretting hand to access notes higher up the neck.

D

delay (echo): On an electric guitar, mimics the echo effect by playing a delayed copy of the original sound.

detuning: Intentionally putting one or more of the strings out of tune for a specific effect.

diatonic: Using the notes of the major scale.

diminished: Intervals decreased in size by a semitone are known as *diminished intervals*. The diminished chord is based on intervals of a minor third, and the so-called diminished scale consists of alternating tones and semitones.

distortion: Change of tone quality, with a harsh sound, achieved by overdriving an amplifier, or the use of a distortion pedal, fuzz box, or overdriver.

double stopping: Forming a chord by stopping two or more strings with the left hand on the frets.

double or (multi) tracking: Recording technique enabling a player to superimpose a number of "takes" of a particular piece.

dreadnought: A large-bodied, steel-strung acoustic guitar.

drone strings: Strings not intended to be played with the fingers, but tuned to vibrate in sympathy with the main instrument's strings.

E

effects: Numerous special effects are possible on a modern electric guitar, including *chorus, compression, delay, distortion, enhancer, expander, flanger, fuzz, harmonizer, Leslie, octave divider, overdrive, panning, preamp, reverb, tremolo, vibrato, volume pedal,* and *wah-wah* (see separate listings for each).

enhancer: On an electric guitar, device to improve sound definition.

expander: The opposite of *compressor*, increasing the range of volume on an electric guitar.

F

F-holes: Violin-style F-shaped sound holes, usually found in pairs.

feedback: The loud whine produced by a microphone or pickup receiving and amplifying its own signal from a loudspeaker.

fill: In jazz and rock, a short melodic figure played by an accompanying instrument between phrases.

fingerpicking: Right-hand technique in which the strings are plucked by individual fingers.

Flamenco: A Spanish style of playing, singing, and dancing. Forms of flamenco include *alegrias, buierias, fandangos, farrucas, ganadinas, malaguena, seguidillas, siguiryas, soleas,* and *tarantas,* and the guitar often interjects *falsetas* (melodic improvised interludes) into these forms. Techniques in flamenco guitar-playing include *alzapua* (up-and-down strokes with the thumbnail), *apagado* (left-hand damping), *golpe* (tapping on the body of the guitar), *picado* (fingerstyle), and *rasqueado* (strumming by unfurling the fingers across the strings).

flanger: On an electric guitar, a chorus-type effect, using a delayed signal with a slight pitch variation.

flat-top: A guitar whose soundboard, or top, is flat.

fretboard: The wooden strip, usually of hardwood, attached atop the neck and into which the frets are set. Also called the *fingerboard.*

frets: Metal wires set into the fretboard at precise distances, allowing the strings to sound the correct pitches along the neck.

folk: The music of rural cultures, usually passed down orally. The word *folk* is also used to describe composed music in the style of true folk music, particularly after the "folk revival" of the 1950s.

free jazz: A jazz style of the 1960s, which is freely improvised without reference to a specific tune or harmonic sequence.

fusion: A jazz-rock fusion, but also any form of "crossover" from one style to another.

fuzz: On an electric guitar, a form of distortion, operated by a fuzz pedal.

G

gig bags: A portable padded bag made of either canvas, nylon, or leather that you can use as an alternative to a hard case. They zip shut and offer about the same protection as a piece of soft leather luggage.

glissando: A slide from one note to another.

grace notes: Short notes played just before the main note of a tune as an ornament.

groove: A repeated rhythmic pattern in jazz and rock.

guitar synthesizer: Guitars with built-in synthesizers for dramatically altering the sound, or equipped with MIDI to control external synthesizers, drum machines, and so on.

H

habafiera: A Cuban dance, or its rhythm.

hammer-on: Notes played by hammering the string with the fingers of the left hand, rather than plucking with the right hand.

harmonics: Notes with an ethereal tone higher than the pitch of the string, produced by lightly touching the string at certain points.

harmonizer: On an electric guitar, a chorus-type effect adding a sound in harmony with the original signal.

head: In jazz, the statement of the tune before and after the improvised solos.

headstock: The structure at the end of the neck that holds the tuning machines.

interval: The distance between two notes. For example, C to G is a fifth (that is, five notes of the scale); C to E is a third (three notes); and C to C is an octave (eight notes).

inversion: see *chords*.

jazz: African-American in origin, characterized by the use of improvisation, "blue notes," and syncopated rhythms.

Latin: Music of Latin-American origin, including dance rhythms such as the *habañera*, samba, rumba, bossa nova, and so on.

legato: Smoothly, not staccato.

Leslie: The Leslie cabinet, originally for use with electronic organs, contains a rotating speaker, giving a swirling effect to music played on an electric guitar.

licks: In jazz and rock, short, almost clichéd, phrases inserted into a solo or used as rills.

machine head: See *tuning peg*.

microtone: Interval of less than a semitone.

MIDI: Musical Instrument Digital Interface. This allows musical instruments such as electric guitars and synthesizers to communicate with sequencers, effects boxes, computers, and so on.

minimalism: A movement in music from the 1960s using static harmonies, repeated patterns, and a minimum of material.

modes: Scales using the notes of the diatonic scale, other than the major and minor scales. The modes, such as Dorian, Phrygian, and Aeolian, originated in medieval music, but were adopted by jazz players in the 1950s.

modulate: Move from one key to another.

N

neck: The long structure that runs from the body to the headstock, and onto which the fretboard is attached. Necks have a longitudinal curve that can be adjusted by means of the truss rod. The width, shape, and curvature of the neck largely determine a guitar's playability.

nut: The notched fitting—usually of bone, ivory, ebony, metal, or plastic—that guides the strings from the fretboard to the tuning pegs.

O

octave divider: On an electric guitar, an early form of *harmonizer*, adding a sound an octave above or below the original signal.

open tuning: Tuning the strings of the guitar to a specific chord, rather than the conventional E-A-D-G-B-E. There are also other nonconventional tunings, such as D-A-D-G-A-D.

overdrive: On an electric guitar, a form of distortion.

overdubs: Parts added to a recording after the original take.

P

panning: On an electric guitar, moving the source of the sound within the stereo field.

partial chords: Chords not using all the strings of the guitar.

passing chords: Chords used "in passing" from one harmony to another, not part of the main harmonic sequence.

pedal note: A repeated bass note that supports a sequence of changing harmonies.

pentatonic: A scale of five, rather than the more usual seven, notes.

phasing: On an electric guitar, playing two identical sounds slightly out of phase with one another.

pick or plectrum: Object used for striking the guitar strings, usually made from plastic.

pickguard: A protective plate on the body of the guitar that protects the top from being scratched by a pick or fingers.

pickup: The device on electric guitars that picks up and transmits the sound of the strings to the amplifier.

pickup switch: Allows pickups to be turned on individually or in various combinations.

potentiometer (pot): A variable resistor used for an electric guitar's volume and tone controls. Amplifiers also have pots.

preamp: With an electric guitar, the preamplifier can be used as a form of tone control, or to boost the signal.

pull-off: A note played by pulling the string with the fingers of the left hand.

R

raga: A scale used in Indian music. There are hundreds of different ragas, many using microtones.

ragtime: An African-American style of music, a precursor of jazz.

reverb: On an electric guitar, this mimics the echo effect, either by a built-in spring reverb or a digital electronic emulation.

rhythm and blues: African-American pop music originating in the late 1940s, the precursor to rock-and-roll.

riff: In jazz and rock, a short, repeated melodic phrase.

rock, rock-and-roll: Rock evolved in the 1950s from rhythm and blues, and in its 1960s form became known simply as *rock*.

rubato: Not strictly in tempo—played freely and expressively.

rumba (rhumba): Afro-Cuban dance.

S

saddle: The fitting that guides the strings over the bridge. Most electric guitars have individual saddles for each string. These can be adjusted to change a string's length and thus intonation.

scales: A series of ascending or descending notes in a specific key, the basis for compositions in the tonal system.

segue: Moving without a break to the next movement, section, or number.

semitone: A half-step, or halftone. The smallest interval in the diatonic scale—for example, the distance between E and F, or B and C.

serial, twelve-tone: Avant-garde compositional method using the twelve notes of the chromatic scale in series, without reference to traditional harmony or tonality.

slide: A style of guitar-playing using bottleneck, where notes and chords slide from one to another.

solid-body: A guitar whose body is made from a solid piece of wood or is a solid lamination. Most electrics are solid bodies; some are semi-hollow.

soundboard: The resonating top of an acoustic guitar.

sound hole: A hole (or holes) in the top of a guitar through which sound is emitted.

staccato: Detached. Staccato notes or chords are short and clipped, not smoothly moving to the next.

straight eights: In jazz, playing *straight eights* means playing exactly on the beat, whereas *swing* indicates that the rhythm should be interpreted more freely. (See also *swing.*)

string-bending: Using the fingers of the left hand to pull a string to one side, "bending" the pitch of the note.

strings: The cords that are plucked to cause vibrations that produce a guitar's sound. Most guitar strings are solid wire or thin wire wrapped around a solid core; classical guitars have nylon and metal-wound nylon strings. A string's thickness (gauge) depends on its position on the guitar and the relative thickness of the entire six-string set.

swap fours: In jazz, when soloists alternate improvisations with one another every four bars.

swing: A style of jazz of the 1940s, mainly for big bands. Also an instruction to play rhythms freely. (See also *straight eights.*)

syncopation: Shifting the accent of a melody off the main beat of the bar—a characteristic of jazz and much rock and pop music.

T

tailpiece: The device that holds the strings' ball ends.

tempo: The underlying speed of a piece of music.

timbre: The tone quality of a sound.

tonal, tonality: Relating to the system of major and minor keys.

tone (whole tone): An interval of two semitones—for example the distance between C and D, or F and G.

tremolo: On an electric guitar, small and rapid variation in the volume of a note. This effect is often confused with *vibrato,* and the tremolo arm or bar is used to bend the pitch of notes on electric guitars.

trill: Rapid alternation between one note and the note above.

truss rod: A metal rod that runs lengthwise through the neck, increasing its strength and allowing adjustment of the longitudinal curve.

truss rod adjusting nut: The part of the truss rod system that can be tightened or loosened to alter rod tension.

tuning pegs: Devices set into the headstock that anchor strings and allow them to be tuned. Each tuning machine consists of a post, a geared mechanism, and a tuning key.

turnaround: In jazz, the harmony under the last phrase of a tune, taking the music back to the beginning for its repeat.

unison: On exactly the same note. For example, on a twelve-string guitar, the pairs of strings are tuned in unison—that is, to the same note. In jazz, the tune of the head is often played by several instruments in unison.

vamps, vamping: Repeated accompanying figure in jazz and popular music before the melody begins.

vibrato: On an electric guitar, small and rapid variation in the pitch of a note.

voicing: The spacing of the notes in a chord.

volume pedal: Means of altering the volume of sound for an electric guitar, useful in creating the "fade-in" effect or as a "swell" pedal.

W

wah-wah: With an electric guitar, the wah-wah pedal controls the relative bass and treble response of a sound. Fully down it has a high treble tone; fully up it emphasizes the bass. The characteristi "wah-wah" sound is achieved by rocking the pedal back and forth.

whole-tone scale: A six-note augmented scale formed entirely of intervals of a whole tone, such as C-D-E-F♯-G♯-A♯.

APPENDIX B

Method Books and Other Music Books

Most of these books are available on Amazon.com and should be readily available in a decent-sized music store:

Mickey Baker, *Mickey Baker's Jazz Guitar* (Omnibus Press).

William Bay, Mike Christiansen, *Mastering the Guitar: A Comprehensive Method for Today's Guitarist* (Mel Bay Publications). This is a seven-book series.

Gene Bertonicini, *Approaching the Guitar* (Kjos Music Co). Amazon.com has misspelled his name as *Bertonzini.*

Mick Goodrich (Pat Metheny, contributor), *The Advancing Guitarist* (Hal Leonard).

Ted Greene, *Modern Chord Progressions* (Warner Bros.).

William G. Leavitt, *Modern Method for the Guitar: Vols 1, 2, 3* (Hal Leonard).

John Mehegan, *Jazz Rhythm and the Improvised Line Jazz Improvisation* (Music Sales Corp).

John Mehegan, *Tonal and Rhythmic Principles Jazz Improvisation* (Music Sales Corp). The Mehegan books are nominally for piano players, but if you can translate the material for the guitar, you will develop fantastic musical muscles.

Frederick M. Noad, *Solo Guitar* (Music Sales Corp).

Aaron Shearer, *Classical Guitar Technique* (Warner Bros.).

Nicolas Slonimsky, *Thesaurus of Scales and Musical Patterns* Music Sales Corp). This was the book that John Coltrane studied extensively.

Tommy Tedesco, *For Guitar Players Only* (Dale Zdenek Publications). This book is out of print, but if you can find it, it's well worth buying. It will help you with your sight reading.

Music Books Authored by Jack Wilkins

Jack Wilkins, Windows Transcriptions (Hal Leonard).
Modern Jazz Greats (Hal Leonard).
Mel Bay Presents 2000 Jazz Guitar (Mel Bay).

APPENDIX C

Guitar Tricks

Hammer-On

This is used a lot in rock, blues, and folk playing. Fret a note with your first finger, say D at the fifth fret, String 5. Now, while the note is still ringing, "hammer down" your finger on E at the seventh fret, String 5, and keep it there.

Pull-Off

This is really a hammer-on in reverse. You need to have both fingers on the fret. Play the note E, as before, then pull off your finger so the D will sound clearly.

Trill

If you rapidly combine both techniques above, you get a trick often used in rock-and-roll that may sound familiar called a *trill*.

String Bends

A lot of rock guitarists and blues guitarists use a string bend. If you pull or push the string, once you've fretted the note, you can actually bend it almost to the note on the next fret. It's the same sort of technique as using a mechanical tremolo arm. It generally works best if you use thin gauge strings.

Double String Bends

A rock and blues cliché, but effective on occasion if the spirit moves you. The trick is to have both fingers in place ahead of time. Here, you play the D, on the seventh fret of String 3, bending it until you've reached the pitch of E, and—while still sounding the bent note—play E on an adjacent string (fifth fret, String 2), letting the two notes ring together.

Another trick is to play the D and E together (major second), fingering them as above, and then bend the D into an E, letting the two Es sound together.

Vibrato

This just means deliberately invoking a "wow-wow" kind of effect. All you do is rock your finger back and forth on the note as you fret it. The more exaggerated the movement of your hand, the broader will be the "vib."

Slide

This is simple. Slide your finger from one fret to another while the note is still ringing.

APPENDIX D

Web Sites
for the Guitar

Jack Wilkins's Web Site

✐ *www.jackwilkins.com*

Curt Sheller—Guitarists Links

✐ *www.curtsheller.com*

One of the best general sites about the guitar for beginners

✐ *http://guitar.about.com/musicperform/guitar*

Guitar at About—Online Guitar Lessons and Jazz Transcriptions

✐ *http://guitar.about.com*

International Online Jazz Guitar Newsletter

✐ *www.musicweb-uk.com*

Guitar Resources on the World Wide Web

✐ *www.cmeabaysection.org/guitres.html*

All JAZZ GUITAR - The Online Community for the Jazz Guitar Enthusiast

✐ *www.mindsync.com/kerin/donprice*

Online Guitar Chord Dictionary

✐ *www.lib.virginia.edu/dmmc/Music/GuitarChords*

***Rolling Stone* magazine's Web page**

✐ *www.rollingstone.com*

Educational Site

✐ *http://VisionMusic.com*

AMG All Music Guide

✐ *www.allmusic.com*

Progression - Playing - Guitar

✐ *www.progression.co.uk/playing*

GuitarSite.com—Home of Guitar News Weekly & the 2000 Guitars Database

✐ *www.guitarsite.com*

Sing Those Songs

✐ *www.mediaversal.com/wesley/songbook.html*

APPENDIX E

More Scales and Chord Shapes

FIGURE APP1:
Major scale
fingerings
(2 Octaves)

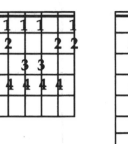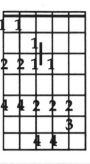

Work out the others for yourself. Practice playing through the cycle of 4ths.

FIGURE APP2:
Minor scale
fingerings

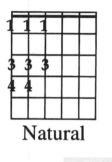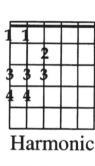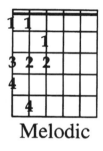

Natural   Harmonic   Melodic

Work these out in 2 octaves.

FIGURE APP3(a):
Pentatonic
scales

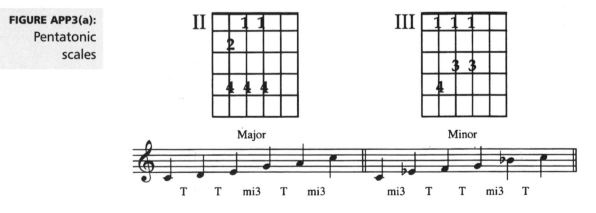

Pentatonic, or 5-note, scales (used widely in blues and rock)
Work these into 2 octaves and practice through the cycle of 4ths.

FIGURE APP3(b):
Augmented
scale

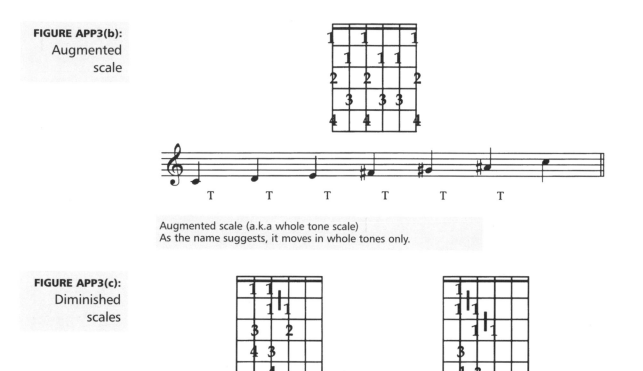

Augmented scale (a.k.a whole tone scale)
As the name suggests, it moves in whole tones only.

FIGURE APP3(c):
Diminished
scales

There are two different types of scales, as shown above.
Work out in 2 octaves and play through the keys.

FIGURE APP3(d): Basic 7th chord shapes

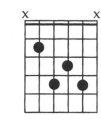 

Maj7 (1573)

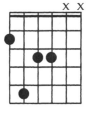 

Maj7+5 (1573)

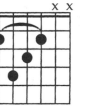 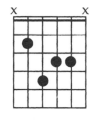

Min Maj7 (1573)

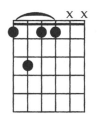 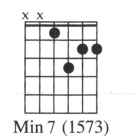

Min 7 (1573)

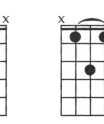 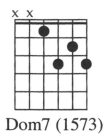

Dom7 (1573)

FIGURE APP3(e):
Basic 7th
chord shapes

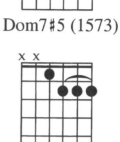

Dom7♯5 (1573)

mi7♭5 (1573)

(Can take its name from any
note in the chord)

Dim7 (1573)

(1573)   Dom7♭5

Dom7♯9 (1573)

FIGURE APP3(f):
Basic 7th
chord shapes

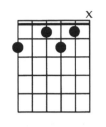

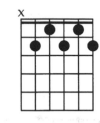

Chord shapes 3   Dom7♭9

FIGURE APP4:
Bourree in
E Minor

Bourree in E Minor

Moderately

O Little Town of Bethlehem

(Arranged by J. Wilkins)

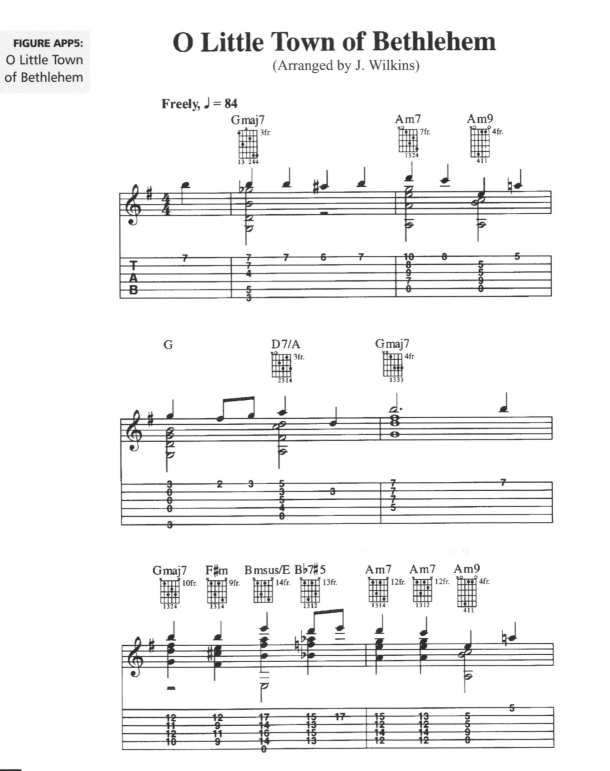

FIGURE APP5:
O Little Town
of Bethlehem

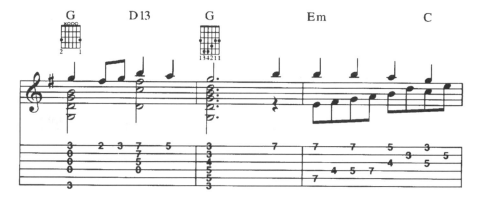

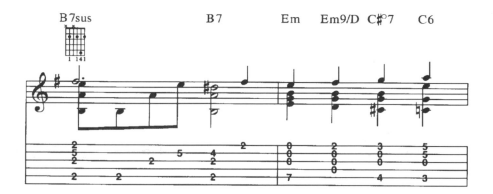

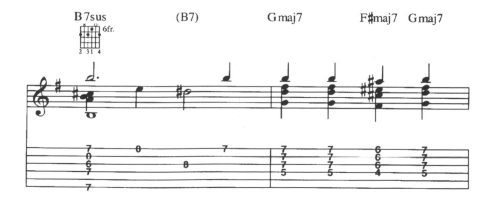

FIGURE APP5:
O Little Town
of Bethlehem

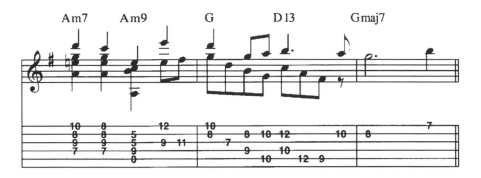

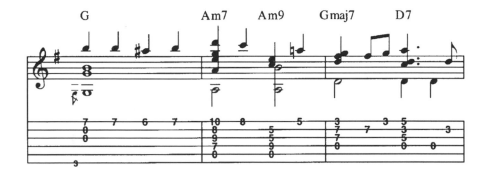

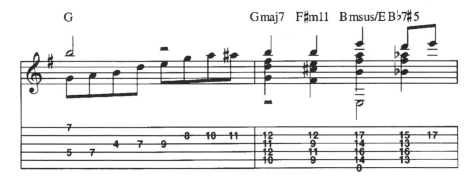

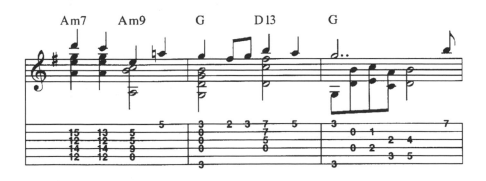

FIGURE APP5:

O Little Town
of Bethlehem

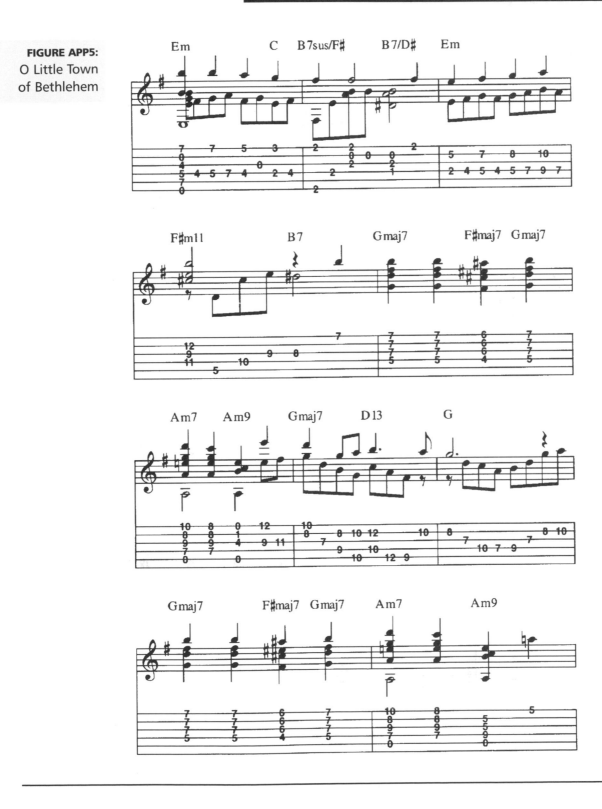

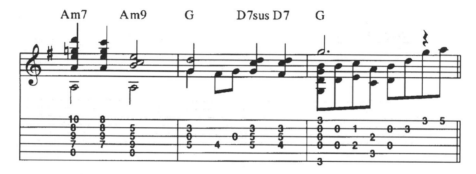

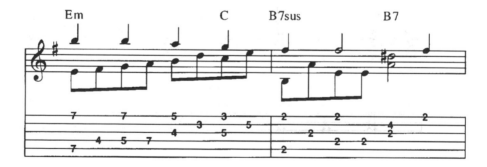

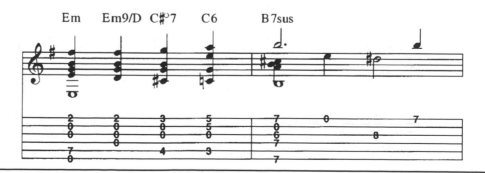

FIGURE APP5:
O Little Town of Bethlehem

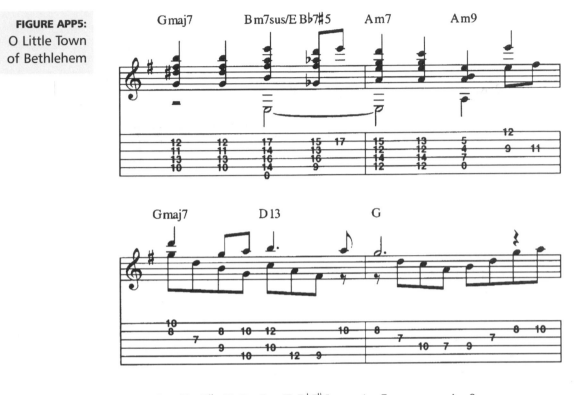

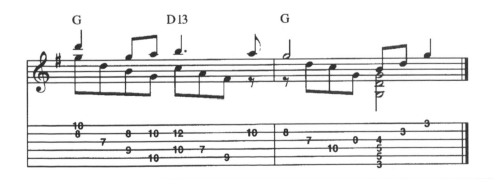

APPENDIX F

Blank Sheet Music

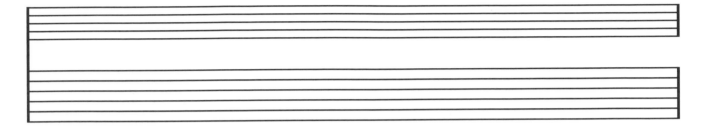

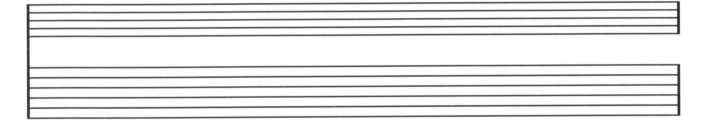

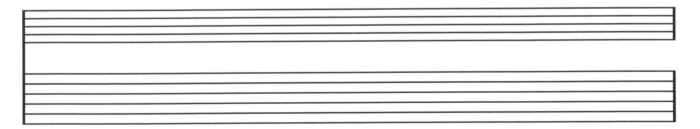

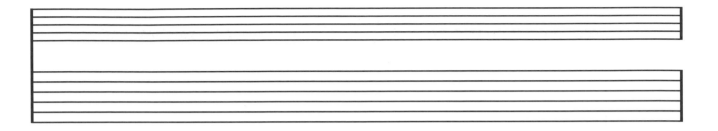

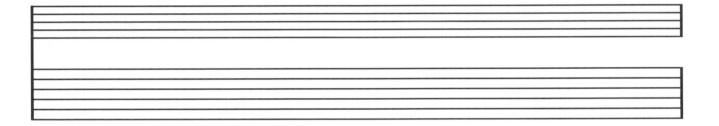

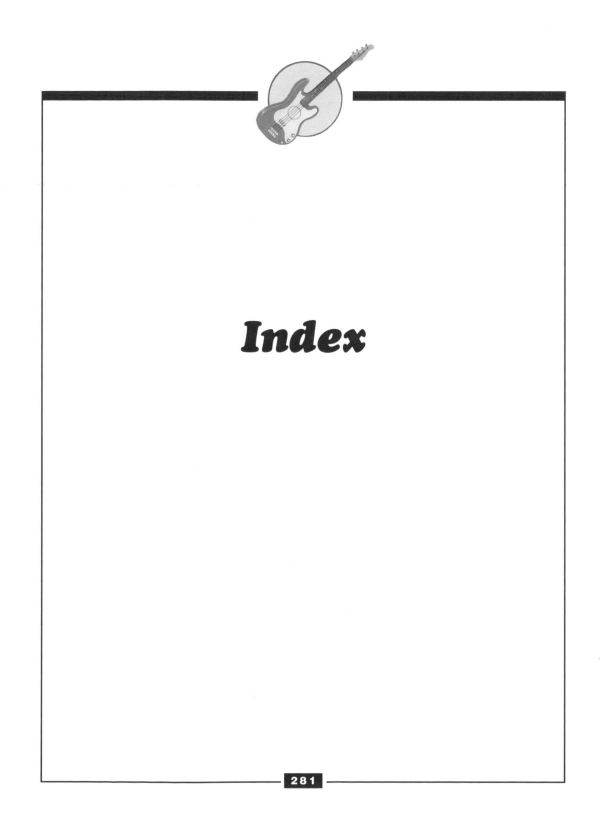

Index

Cut time, 174
Cycle of fourths and fifths,
   235–36

D

"Dark as a Dungeon," 62
Davis, Miles, 53
Debussy, 226
Deep Purple, 73
DeFranco, Buddy, 48, 50
De Johnette, Jack, 54
Delay, 115
Delmore Brothers, 61
De Lucia, Paco, 10, **24**
De Lucia, Pepe, 24
Derek and the Dominos, 69
Der mynnen regein, 14
Desmond, Paul, 50
DeStefano, Lorenzo, 48
Diatonic chords, 235
DiFranco, Ani, 66
Digital audio tape (DAT), 121
Digital sampling, 121
DiMeola, Al, 24
Diminishing, 228
Discipline, 73
Distortion, 116
The Doc Watson Family, 58
Double string bends,
   256–66
Dowland, John, 226
Downstrokes, 158, 188
Drew, Kenny, Jr., 54
Drifting Pioneers, 61
D-shaped sound hole, 42

Dumas, Alexandre, 9
Dunn, Blind Willie, 37
Durham, Eddie, 12, 43
DVDs, 121
Dylan, Bob, 79
Dynamic markings, 181

E

EADGBE (tuning), 6
Echo, 116
Edwards, Honeyboy, 34
Effects pedals, 117–18
Electric guitars, 43, 60, **69,** 81,
   88, 90
   changing strings on, 103
   early development, 10–12
   first commercial, 11–12
   history of, 14–15
   problems with, 108
   solid-bodied, 12–13
   sound from, 110–11
   volume, 11
Electric Ladyland, 71
Electronic effects, 115–16
Electro Spanish guitar, 11
Electro String Company, 11,
   15, 111
El Hombre, 52
Ellington, Duke, 40, 41, 53, 226
Ellis, Herb, 48, 55
Ellison, Ralph, 42, 43
"El Maestro," 4, 14
Engineer, 122
Enharmonic notes, 201
Eno, Brian, 72

Epiphone Les Paul guitar,
   70, 81
"Escape," 75
Espinel, Vicente, 14
Evans, Bill, 51
Evening Star, 72
Everly, Don, 61
Everly, Ike, 61
Everly, Phil, 61
Everly Brothers, 60
Exposure, 73

F

Falla, Manual de, 22
Falsetas, 9
Farlow, Tal, **47–48,** 49, 50, 55
Farmer, Art, 50
Feldman, Victor, 51
Fender, Leo, 12, 111, 112
Fender Bassman amplifier, 38
Fender Broadcaster, 12
Fender Electrical Instrument
   Company, 12
Fender Stratocaster guitars, 38,
   70, 79, 80, 82, 112
Fender Telecaster guitars, 12,
   15, 82, 112
Fender Twin Reverb, 112
Fenton, Nick, 45
F holes, 35, 59, 79
Fingerboard, 86
Fingerpicking, 192–93
Fingerstyle, 139–40
Fingertips, nails versus,
   8, 19